T0286956

Cambridge Elements ≡

Elements in Psychology and Culture
edited by
Kenneth D. Keith
University of San Diego

IN SEARCH OF INTEGRITY

A Life-Journey across Diverse Contexts

Robert Serpell
University of Zambia Professor Emeritus

CAMBRIDGE
UNIVERSITY PRESS

Shaftesbury Road, Cambridge CB2 8EA, United Kingdom

One Liberty Plaza, 20th Floor, New York, NY 10006, USA

477 Williamstown Road, Port Melbourne, VIC 3207, Australia

314–321, 3rd Floor, Plot 3, Splendor Forum, Jasola District Centre,
New Delhi – 110025, India

103 Penang Road, #05–06/07, Visioncrest Commercial, Singapore 238467

Cambridge University Press is part of Cambridge University Press & Assessment,
a department of the University of Cambridge.

We share the University's mission to contribute to society through the pursuit of
education, learning and research at the highest international levels of excellence.

www.cambridge.org
Information on this title: www.cambridge.org/9781009523844

DOI: 10.1017/9781009523813

First published 2024

A catalogue record for this publication is available from the British Library.

ISBN 978-1-009-52384-4 Hardback
ISBN 978-1-009-52382-0 Paperback
ISSN 2515-3986 (online)
ISSN 2515-3943 (print)

Cambridge University Press & Assessment has no responsibility for the persistence
or accuracy of URLs for external or third-party internet websites referred to in this
publication and does not guarantee that any content on such websites is, or will
remain, accurate or appropriate.

In Search of Integrity

A Life-Journey across Diverse Contexts

Elements in Psychology and Culture

DOI: 10.1017/9781009523813
First published online: March 2024

Robert Serpell
University of Zambia Professor Emeritus
Author for correspondence: Robert Serpell, robertnserpell@gmail.com

Abstract: This Element traces the origins of an individual's philosophical orientation and the processes by which it was elaborated over the course of his life-journey. The author discusses how selected stories from his personal experience reflect the intimate culture of a particular social group of which he was a participant member at the time. The author's life-journey includes a tumultuous period of emerging adulthood in Singapore and Oxford. Moving to Zambia in 1965 aged twenty-one, he conducted research, teaching, and writing including sojourns in England and in Maryland, USA. He discusses how his perspective in cultural psychology relates to his personal life as a migrant and as a parent, and to his views on how the world can best address the challenges of cooperative communication in the 2020s.

This Element also has a video abstract:
www.Cambridge.org/EPAC_Serpell_abstract

Keywords: cultural psychology, developmental narrative, parenting, human development, Africa

ISBNs: 9781009523844 (HB), 9781009523820 (PB), 9781009523813 (OC)
ISSNs: 2515-3986 (online), 2515-3943 (print)

Contents

Preface

The initial stimulus for composing this autobiography came from Francois Rochat. I am grateful to him for persisting and for his insightful comments on an earlier draft. I am also grateful to Kenneth Keith for encouraging me to complete the project and to the two anonymous referees who read the manuscript and made constructive suggestions for its enhancement. The 'fieldwork' reported in Sections 2 and 3 was generated over an extended period since 2020 with generous assistance on points of factual detail from my sister Hilary Nias and my friend Simon Mollison. My life-journey was influenced by interactions with many individuals. My selection of which of them to name was guided by the structure of the story I have reconstructed from a combination of recollection and reasoning. Where my appraisal of those interactions is negative, I have sought to follow the principle of avoiding hostile attribution of motives to persons still alive. Responsibility for the decisions I took along the way remains my own. In Sections 5–8, the narrative of my research endeavours at the interface between human development and culture is documented with citations to publications between 1965 and 2020 that explicitly acknowledge the contributions of my many collaborators.

The period of my life discussed in Sections 2–8 begins when I was six years old in 1950 and ends when I was about seventy in 2014. My conjugal partnership with my wife Namposya not only informed the co-construction of our intimate family culture, and our socialisation of our children. It sustained a pattern of reciprocal support grounded in loyalty and honesty. Her companionship often sensitised me to latent biases in my intuitive sense of what was right, or funny, or absurd. Our differences of intuition were always open for debate, and she always took my considered opinions seriously, however radically unconventional they might appear. Her effortless generosity and personal warmth opened many doors for me, in ways I came to appreciate even more in retrospect after her death. In 2015, Namposya fell seriously ill with uterine cancer, and I took extended leave from my professional work to travel abroad with her for treatment, until she died in December 2016. Deciding not to include events and experiences after 2014 in this Element was a conscious decision, based on recognition that since then I have entered a different phase of my life-journey.

1 Personal Development in Sociocultural Context

This Element can be read in three complementary ways: as an autobiographical memoir of my personal life-journey, as a case-study of engagement with sociocultural changes over time across several societies, or as an interpretive bid to understand the relation between those two stories in terms of a situated theoretical framework for the study of human development in sociocultural context.

Scattered across the sections, I reflect on some broad philosophical commitments that have served to guide my search for an integrative account of my personal development across various sociocultural contexts: inclusion and tolerance; rejecting interpersonal violence; aesthetic appreciation; forming intimate relationships of trust; and taking responsibility. I do not claim, like Mohandas Gandhi (1927) or Frederick Douglass (1882), that explicit principles served as pillars on which to construct the edifice of a coherent life. The overarching principles that now stand out for me as core personal values emerged gradually over the course of smaller projects situated in particular contexts and can only be convincingly presented with respect to those contexts.

My Personal Life-Journey

I was born into a liberal-minded English family near the end of World War II and grew up in a middle-class suburb of London together with my mother, father and elder sister, commuting by public transport into central London where I was enrolled for my basic schooling in a French-medium Lycee modelled on the standard form of public education in France. Drawing on correspondence in later life with my sister, I reflect in Section 2 on how our parents formulated their interventions in my developmental trajectory. My ensuing life-journey took me to Westminster boarding school in central London for most of my adolescence, to Singapore as an emerging adult in 1961, to Oxford University as an undergraduate student from 1962 to 1965, and then to Lusaka, the capital of newly independent Zambia, where I joined the first academic staff of the University of Zambia (UNZA). In Lusaka my first marriage brought into the world my son, Derek, and launched my career of parenting. After the collapse of that marriage, I met my future wife, Namposya, with whom I partnered over the next 43 years in the delights and challenges of parenting my son Derek, her niece Mwila, our three biological progeny, Zewe, Chisha, and Namwali, and our adopted daughter Suwi. In 1979, at the age of 35, I was granted citizenship of Zambia, and renounced my citizenship of the UK.

Most of my professional life was framed by the University of Zambia (UNZA), progressing up the ranks from junior Research Fellow in 1965 to Full Professor in 1981, serving two spells as Head of the Psychology Department and a six-year stint as Director of the Institute for African Studies. From 1989 to 2003, I relocated with my family to the USA where for twelve years I was a tenured professor at the University of Maryland Baltimore County (UMBC) and Director of a graduate study programme in Applied Developmental Psychology. During that sojourn in the USA, I was granted the status of Resident Alien (green card), which expired on my return to Zambia as Vice-Chancellor of UNZA. After a four-year spell of administration as Vice-Chancellor, I returned to my intellectual home base in the Psychology Department as Professor and Coordinator of graduate studies, devoting much of my effort to international collaboration. In 2019, at the age of seventy-five, I took formal retirement from UNZA, continuing as an independent scholar to write for publication and occasionally contributing to teaching or mentoring.

Family Background

My mother, Estelle had grown up as an only child with her mother and stepfather, first in Western Canada (where she was born in 1917), then from the age of ten in Sussex, England, where she was enrolled in a private school for girls in Seaford. She was the first woman in her family of origin to receive a formal tertiary education, graduating from the University of London's Bedford College with a BA degree in English in 1938. English poetry, plays, and novels were leading sources of inspiration for her and they featured prominently in our family life. She was especially devoted to Shakespeare's plays, but also took a keen interest in modern theatre and in women's emancipation. I realised late in life that the idea of tertiary education had also been part of my grandmother's imagination, inspired by her father's transformative experience of it in his own life in the nineteenth century, and that she had wanted in her youth to be trained as a doctor, but had been denied the opportunity on grounds of gender stereotype. During my childhood I saw quite a bit of Granny but I never became aware of that side of her. It was in conversation with my mother in her nineties reflecting on the character and development of her long deceased mother that I eventually became aware of a strand of intergenerational communication and experiences that had been veiled from me. Estelle was strongly committed to philanthropic charity and gave generously of her time to voluntary local social work with the elderly and the poor. She also maintained a part-time teaching career, mostly in the form of non-vocational evening classes for adults.

My father Michael (known to us as Pa) first met Estelle in London just before the outbreak of World War II, and they were married in 1940, after a short engagement, just as the Blitz attacks on London were beginning. At that time he was working as an assistant curator in the National Portrait Gallery, having graduated from Oxford University's Exeter College with a BA degree in History in 1936. His leading sources of inspiration were European paintings and architecture, and the origins of English parliamentary democracy in the sixteenth and seventeenth centuries. In addition to a love of English literature, my parents shared an admiration for the classical music and literature of France and Germany. Michael had grown up in the north of England, in the city of Leeds, where he was born in 1915, the third of five children of Harold, a graduate of

Oxford university and schoolteacher of German and French at Leeds Grammar School. His mother Katharine graduated in 1908 from Melbourne university in Australia and won a prize in History, but that pioneering achievement was not revealed to us by Pa, who seldom shared with us memories of his childhood. His elder brother, Christopher (who worked for the BBC) lived with his family in Rome and Washington during the 1950s. I got to know them better in my adolescent years while a boarder at Westminster School, after my parents had moved abroad. During my childhood years in Barnes, Pa was the family bread-winner, working from 9 to 5 as a civil servant. His position in the War Office was secret and never discussed in the family.

A Theoretical Framework for the Study of Human Development in Sociocultural Context

Interface between Ontogenetic Change and Historical–Cultural Change

The term **development** is often applied both to sequences of change in the life of an individual (*ontogenesis*) and also to sequences of change in the culture of a group, a society, or a nation over the course of history. But the nature of those sequences of change is quite different in the domain of culture from those termed developmental in the domain of individual ontogenesis. Historical sequences are governed by a convergence of factors, some of them biological as postulated in Darwin's theory of evolution and principles of ecological adaptation, others sociocultural such as international conflicts and revolutions. Some social theorists have suggested that historical changes in society are driven by an overarching process of progress, driven by 'class struggle', 'market forces', or the construc-tion of 'a more perfect union'. In my view there is little benefit in postulating such unifying themes, although I recognise that they resonate with the personal intu-itions of many leading minds. The contemporary terminology of the United Nations that classifies some nations as 'under-developed' or 'developing' is useful for aggregating countries or regions in terms of certain, largely economic criteria. But it is less informative for systematic understanding of social change than more narrowly focused terms such as industrialised, institutionalised, egali-tarian, etc. I use the expression 'progressive social change' advisedly, situating each such sequence of events in relation to a particular contextual framework.

The Eco-Cultural Niche of Child Development

The Western academic disciplines of social anthropology and developmental psychology converged in the late twentieth century on the influential idea that the way in which a child develops is adapted to the demands of a particular niche

(Super & Harkness, 1986; Gallimore et al., 1989), some aspects of which arise from the physical ecosystem (**settings**) inhabited by the community into which the child is born, while others are constructed socioculturally over time by that community (**practices**). Children are said to be 'socialised' in particular ways that reflect implicit beliefs, held by parents or other authoritative members of the community, known as **ethnotheories**. Bronfenbrenner's (1979) influential **ecological theory** provided a systemic account of human development in sociocultural context, which he revised in 2005 to situate a given cultural group's developmental niche within a **chronosystem** that changes over the course of history. The chronosystems of different human societies around the world underwent transformative global integration over the course of the nineteenth and twentieth centuries. The diffusion of Western culture through Christian proselytization and imperial domination has attracted critical attention under the heading of **cultural hegemony** (Gramsci, 1992; Apple, 2014). Scientific accounts of the contemporary global crisis of climate change have raised public awareness around the world of the interconnectedness of human activity with other forms of life that share the same environment, and with physical processes that mediate changes over time in the world as we know it, with dire implications for the next generation of humans (Sanson, van Hoorn & Burke, 2019).

Intimate Culture

The socialisation (or enculturation) experienced by a given child depends on characteristics of the niche in which she grows up, such as the locally prevalent physical and social settings, traditional practices, and ethnotheories of a particular community. However, even within those eco-cultural constraints, variations can often be detected between families. For instance, two families in a given neighbourhood may differ in adherence to a particular religion or in their connection to other social organisations such as an economic enterprise or a political activity. In one family 'growing up well' includes saying one's prayers; in another it includes helping out in the family business. The notion of an intimate family culture was initially inspired by the proposal that a 'family code' constitutes a set of factors 'intermediate between the cultural influences [on child development] and individual interaction patterns. This code is not a set of stable enduring characteristics, but is an evolving regulatory system' (Sameroff & Fiese, 1992, pp. 357–358), that includes family routines and paradigms. I define intimate culture as a systemic constellation of facts, beliefs, and practices shared by a particular group and authoritatively understood by **members** of the group, by virtue of their experience as **insiders** and **owners**. The intimate culture of a social group provides an architectural framework that, looking inwards, affords constraints and opportunities for behaviour and development, and generates a sense of belonging ('I am a member') mediated by a sense of ownership of the system of meanings that informs its distinctive recurrent activities. This psycho-social orientation towards a culture is what I consider to be a key feature of cultural identity (Serpell, 2017). Looking outwards, it represents a particular social group's distinctive character. Several levels of grouping can be distinguished, such as neighbourhoods, church congregations, and families. 'Any particular intimate culture will include traces of ... larger incorporating social formations, but will filter them selectively' (Serpell, 2001, p. 251). In later sections, I discuss the intimate culture of my family of origin (Section 2), my peer group in secondary school (Section 3), undergraduate student life at university (Section 4), and various clusters of academic colleagues (Sections 5–8).

Institutionalised Public Basic Schooling

Many cultural traditions include in their ethnotheories of child development and socialisation an activity known as education, whereby authorised cultural insiders explicitly transmit traditional knowledge and train children to conform with traditional practices. The range of behaviour covered by formal education and its curriculum and instructional methods varies widely across traditions. One particular model of Institutionalised Public Basic Schooling (IPBS) originated in Western Europe in the nineteenth century and has become very widely dispersed around the world in the twentieth century, driven by several social, political, and economic factors (Serpell & Hatano, 1997). This model is often treated by social scientists and public policymakers as a standard. Thus, the global advocacy movement known as Education for All (UNESCO, 1990) was widely operationalised in terms of access to school, implicitly defined as IPBS. But attending school is just one of the many systems of activity that are interdependent and embedded within multiple layers of organisation (Bronfenbrenner, 1979, 2005). When schooling is examined as part of a system, it becomes clear that the linkages between a society's economy and the particular skills taught in schools vary at multiple levels and change over time.

Biculturation

The notion that an individual can become, or aspire to become, competent in more than one culture has been studied as an aspect of *acculturation* (adapting to a new culture; Sam, 1997), typically with reference to international migrants. Others have focused on it as part of the development of *personal identity* (Boykin, 1985; Phinney & Devich-Navarro, 1997) typically with reference to marginalised groups, and of *cultural blending*, typically with reference to families of mixed heritage. Blending has often been portrayed as problematic, but has acquired more positive connotations in the contexts of multicultural politics and cosmopolitanism (Sam et al., 2013). I have been impressed by the idea that there is a sensitive period in human development for incorporation of a cultural meaning system, related to an individual's emerging sense of a 'psychological interior' (Minoura, 1992). One important psychological dimension of the relationship with a particular culture is the degree to which an individual feels accepted as a member of the group and the related degree to which s/he feels ownership of the culture's system of meanings. A person who feels confident that s/he is a member of a cultural group can claim authority to explain to an outsider the meaning of a concept or practice distinctive to that group. The developmental process of increasing membership/ownership of a culture has been captured with the theoretical expression of 'participatory appropriation' (Rogoff, 1993; Serpell, 1993b). The emergence of my own 'psychological interior' in adolescence is described in Section 3, and the significance of 'participatory appropriation' in my emerging adulthood in Section 4.

Multilingualism

I use the term **plurilingual** to designate an individual who is at least bilingual and may have a command of three or more languages. My understanding of multilingualism was significantly deepened in the 1970s and beyond by encountering the field of sociolinguistics. The colloquial use of the term **dialect** to refer to a **nonstandard** variety of a language (e.g., Cockney is a dialect of English) gave way in academic discourse to the more detached view that most natural languages in the real world have some internal diversity in which any variety with internal consistency of form is designated a dialect. Thus, Cockney, Yorkshire, and Oxford/Queen's English are three among many dialects of English, including Zambian English, Nigerian English, Jamaican English, Black English Vernacular (also known as Ebonics and African-American Vernacular English), among others.

The normative connotations of colloquial usage were influentially parsed by Ferguson (1959), who coined the term **diglossia** in a landmark study of four nations, to denote the socially stratified usage of two distinct varieties of a language within a single society, where all members are expected to be familiar with both varieties and with the conventions governing their systematic selection for different types of activity or context. For instance, in the 1950s English society regarded the Oxford/Queen's variety as the official standard for use in the contexts of education and broadcasting, and accorded it a higher social status than other varieties. That convention has changed over secular time and is no longer definitive of English culture, let alone of the English-speaking world (Pride, 1983). In Zambia, academic discourse has evolved over the last five decades from describing the society as highly fragmented into more than seventy languages towards consensus that it includes about ten widely spoken Bantu languages, each of which comprises several identifiable dialects. Seven of these have long been designated as official, each in a particular region, and two of them (Bemba and Nyanja) are widely recognised as urban *lingua francas*. The exogenous language English, introduced in the colonial era, remains superposed over all the other speech varieties, commanding overwhelming national power for legislation, higher education and international communication.

The sociolinguistic writings of Gumperz (1977) alerted me to the prevalence of **code-switching** in plurilingual discourse, whereby an individual speaker starts an utterance in one code (e.g., speech variety, dialect) and then continues in another code without losing intelligibility to her interlocutor who shares familiarity with both codes. The motivation for such switches has received considerable analytical attention, culminating in the relatively recent concept of **translanguaging** (Garcia & Wei, 2014; Cummins, 2019), which seeks to honour usage of a multilingual person's full linguistic repertoire, instead of trying to keep narrowly focused on a single language at a time. Many plurilingual speakers around the world acknowledge that language mixing is common in their speech community and reject the suggestion, by some strong advocates of adherence to standards, that it is simply erroneous. The importance of my own plurilingualism as a resource of cross-cultural communication and social integration features in Section 2 as a source of tension among participants in my family of origin, and in Sections 5 and 6 as a foundation for my participatory appropriation of additional languages and empathetic integration into new sociocultural contexts in Zambian society.

Egalitarian discourse has been characterised by Habermas (1975, 1984) as an epistemological underpinning of democratic governance. Put simply, it means that in a conversation between two people, they should ideally be regarded as having equal rights to make any logically possible discourse move, such as questioning or rejecting as implausible any statement made by the other party. In the intimate culture of our family in the 1950s, I recall it being an implicit ideal that we children were allowed, if not encouraged, to invoke when conversing with our adult parents about matters of an abstract nature such as the meaning or spelling of a word, or the existence of God. It was understood that such matters were open for debate, and no one person was an absolute authority. Even the dictionary would often offer a number of alternative meanings for a given word, and examples of their usage. As for God, the concept was mysterious, and neither the Bible nor a priest could be relied upon to fully explain it. Later in my life, the principle of egalitarian discourse became a guiding principle of my research seeking to understand the child-rearing practices and values of families in Zambia (Section 6) and in the USA (Section 7).

Research Methodology

During my second year of high school, when I was fourteen, I started keeping a diary explicitly intended only for myself. Inscriptions on the front page of each volume read: 'This book is PRIVATE. Please leave it alone'. I continued the practice across several volumes until I was eighteen and added a further volume at a time of emotional crisis when I was twenty. Before revisiting its contents in old age, I recalled that much of what I wrote had focused on my personal emotions and my interpersonal relationships, on beauty, and on religion. As I prepared to revisit this collection of my thoughts in adolescence that I had not even opened in the past fifty years, I felt a sense of excitement and foreboding. Part of me was afraid that the immaturity of my reflections would be so overwhelming as to make me feel completely alienated from the person I had been. Yet I hoped that re-reading them might give me some insight into the ways in which my intellectual and personal developments were intertwined. When I finally summoned up the courage to open these scruffy little notebooks, I discovered that they included evidence of formative experiences that I had completely forgotten. I was surprised to find that a lot of the text in volume one was written in French, a language I had little opportunity to use orally in that period of my life. I was also surprised to rediscover a connection between what I was learning in class about Latin and Greek philosophy and poetry and my private reflections on life as I knew it at first hand. In citing selected passages from the diaries, I have retained the original wording, in the tradition of my earlier, ethnographic reports (Serpell, 1993a; Serpell, Baker & Sonnenschein, 2005). In transcribing my own words from the diaries I kept in the 1950s and 1960s, I have tried to discipline myself to treat the voice of that younger me with the same respect, as an auto-ethnographer.

In this Element, the style of writing in my narrative accounts of phases in my personal development alternates between the academic style of this introduction and informal storytelling infused with emotion and humour. I hope readers will agree with me that those dimensions of storytelling belong in this Element. The orthography I have followed for Bantu languages is that advocated by Banda et al. (2008).

Preview of Sections to Follow

Sections 2 and 3 focus respectively on early phases of my life journey (childhood and adolescence). In each phase, I was embedded in a culturally structured social niche (family home, high school) characterised by a distinctive system of practices and meanings that I experienced transactionally through an intimate culture. I discuss what I learned in each phase about certain transcendent philosophical values illustrated by critical experiences – sometimes with a companion, sometimes alone.

In Section 3, I reflect on the emergence of my 'psychological interior' during adolescence, and how my emerging identity selectively appropriated the classical perspective of Western culture inspiringly conveyed by my admired teacher, Theo Zinn. Then, in Sections 4 and 5, I discuss how those issues were elaborated in a period of emerging adulthood, often sparked by a project for a certain purpose, but nudged into various twists and turns along the way: **inclusion and tolerance**; **rejecting interpersonal violence**; **aesthetic appreciation**; **forming intimate relationships of trust**; and **taking responsibility**. I hope thereby to throw some new light on how and why perspectives on those issues differ so greatly among individual interpreters of the human condition, across societies, and across cultures. In Sections 6 and 7, I discuss two themes of my systematic research conducted between 1973 and 2020, and consider how they reflect and perhaps illuminate critical experiences in my personal, adult life: **learning to listen respectfully**, and **exploring different ways of knowing** (languages, disciplines, research methods, cultural systems, translanguaging). In Section, 8 I discuss how engagement with progressive social change strengthened my commitment to **perspectivism**, a philosophical framework for situated understanding, and to **bridging,** a strategic approach to peaceful intercultural coexistence, that I consider a crucial requirement for progressive, global social change. My overarching goal is to articulate a perspective on the contemporary world that I seek to explain as having emerged over the course of an individual life journey as I travelled across various spatial and sociocultural contexts over time, impacted and inspired by interactions with salient persons in events, episodes, and contexts that are all interconnected within a multi-layered, dynamic system.

2 The Intimate Family Culture of My Childhood Home (London 1951–1957)

One day, when I was about seven, I ran away from home. I don't remember why. But I remember vividly listening to the anxious voice of my father calling out for me, as I crouched in the dark in the bushes at the end of our road. Across from those bushes was the beginning of Barnes common, a favourite place for walks with the family dog, with trees and grass and a pond. I had toyed with the idea of hiding there, but hadn't got that far when my concerned father came out looking for me, calling my name in the dark. Whatever it was that had prompted my escape gave way to a sense of obligation to assuage his evident anxiety. So I stood up and we walked together back home.

Home was a safe place where I belonged, peopled by my family: Mummy, Pa, Hicky (my elder sister) and me (known as Robbie, and later Rob), plus the family dog, Kitson (see Figures 1 and 3). Together we owned a system of meanings that informed our everyday practices and a unique family tradition, including beliefs about our relations with the wider world. As I grew older, my understanding of that family's intimate culture and my position in it expanded and deepened. The idea that our family had its own distinctive culture was expressed in a variety of ways, including the social geography of our physical residence – what cultural psychologists have referred to as *the developmental niche* (Super & Harkness, 1986) or, more precisely, the *eco-cultural niche of child development* (Gallimore et al., 1989). While much of it could be characterised as a middle-class 1950s English way of life, our parents emphasised its distinctiveness through particular recurrent activities and cherished family stories, that were only fully understood by the four of us individuals who constituted our family.

Our Kitson Road house had a well-defined, internal social geography: *upstairs*, along the back wall of the house, Hicky and I each had our own separate bedroom where we slept at night, did our homework for school, and played various games and hobbies. This floor also included a communal bathroom and lavatory and a spare bedroom, sometimes occupied by a live-in helper known as an 'au pair'. These were young women originating from various European countries (France, Germany, Sweden) who received free accommodation in exchange for some childminding and housekeeping duties, and were expected to learn by immersion how to converse in English. In the front of the house, separated from the back by the stairwell, was our parents' bedroom. We children were only allowed into it at designated times, one of which was Sunday morning, when, after a period protected for them to 'sleep in', we were invited to join them for their morning tea. Conversation on those mornings was warm and humorous, often playful with words, with recourse to the dictionary to resolve disagreements. One dimension of communication that was strictly regulated from above in our intimate family culture in Barnes was the use of expletives. 'Swear words' were not allowed to be used in the family.

Downstairs was also divided into compartments, each dedicated to particular activities. The core of our family life was located in the kitchen, where a coal stove known as 'the boiler', functioned as the family hearth, and a large square table served as the gathering point for breakfast and supper, as well as Sunday lunch. The kitchen was also the designated sleeping space for Kitson in his basket on the floor, and the storage space for Mummy's academic and professional documents on a shelf along one wall, known as 'on the side'. When the documents were not in use, they were normally shrouded with a counterpane. Leading off the kitchen was a narrow 'scullery' that housed a gas cooker and

Figure 1 Robbie, Mummy, Hicky, and Kitson outside our house
in Barnes – early 1950s.

a sink for washing-up after meals. Next to the kitchen was the sitting room, which was normally reserved for entertaining visitors, furnished with a suite facing an open hearth that was only rarely lit with a coal fire. Beyond the suite was a bow window opening onto the back garden. Pa's study was located at the front of the house. The front and back gardens were small, walled enclosures about 5 meters square, planted with minimal vegetation. I was once allocated a 'plot', about 50 cm square, in which to grow vegetables as a hobby, and I proudly watched the carrots I planted sprout. The front garden was reserved for flowers, including a large magnolia shrub.

The Parents

Unlike the middle-class British or American childhood homes of many of my contemporaries, ours included no television and no car. Our mother Estelle once confirmed in her old age to Hicky that she and Pa had construed their child-rearing of us as a project of cultural enrichment with an agenda that they had discussed and planned when we children were still very young. I think this enculturation curriculum was something that Estelle and Michael created together as a couple, and derived joint pleasure in putting into practice. Theirs was a love affair deeply imbued with aesthetic and ethical appreciation of literature, and guiding their children into that world was an inherently gratifying shared agenda. Mummy and Pa always presented themselves to us children as an integral 'parental unit' on matters of discipline, but often it was only one of them who spent time with me on a planned activity, with or without my sister. It was mainly Pa who escorted me to the toy shop to choose a new toy soldier, Mummy who showed me how to check and repair a fuse in the basement. When I was a little older, it was Pa who took me to visit art galleries, and Mummy who took me on visits to the Old People's Home where she did voluntary service. Cooking was Mummy's domain, in which she supervised my occasional peripheral contributions such as cutting or stirring some ingredients or lifting a cooked item out of the oven with mittens.

On Sunday mornings, Pa took Hicky and me and Kitson for a long walk, usually along the river Thames towpath, while Mummy stayed home to prepare lunch. We often paused at a pub, where Pa would drink a pint of beer, seated outside in the sun, while we children consumed fizzy drinks and potato crisps. The whole walk lasted about an hour. Conversation was fluid, ranging from observations on the people and dogs we passed along the way, to historical and aesthetic aspects of the buildings, recent events in the children's school lives, and quizzes about geography, arithmetic, or spelling. The Sunday walk was explicitly framed as an entertaining activity and as a healthy form of physical exercise – especially for the dog, and for Pa, whose sedentary office work routine placed him at risk for obesity. Although much of it was implicitly informed by a pedagogical agenda, overall it was understood as a valued family event, expressing and enjoying social solidarity: we, the children, were there to be with Pa as a unique and exclusive group. When we got home, Sunday lunch was served with more than usual decorum, Pa carving a joint of mutton and serving slices onto each person's plate. Routinely, after lunch was time for 'washing-up' the dishes and cutlery, sometimes performed by Pa, with the children 'drying up' and putting them away, excluding Mummy as a reward for cooking the meal while the rest of us were out having fun.

Family Stories

Many of our family's treasured stories were about Kitson, his misbehaviour or charming eccentricities. Kitson was acknowledged by all of us humans as an integral member of the family. He was a black Labrador, extremely docile and received a lot of gentle petting from all four of us, as well as commanding regular attention in the form of taking him for a walk. Other stories in the repertoire of our family's intimate culture centred on conspicuous behaviour, usually aberrant, by one or another family member: *Hicky's screaming fit* as an infant silenced by Mummy's dowsing her in the garden with a bucketful of water; *Rob's arrival home in a Black Mariah police van* (thanks to a kind officer who took pity on Rob when he had overstayed at the swimming pool until after dusk, having cycled there by daylight on a bike which had no lights). 'Bunchananan' was allegedly my youthful pronunciation of the name Buchanan in a conversation with my uncle Richard who was testing my emerging literacy by asking me to read aloud the names displayed on various shop fronts. When he tried to correct me, the story went, I indignantly retorted: 'Well, I call it Bunchananan'. Humour was a common feature of family conversation.

Growth of a Bilingual Orientation

In a gesture celebrating our European cultural identity, our parents enrolled both Hicky and me for our primary schooling in the *Lycee Francais de Londres*, where we acquired fluency in the French language and an insider-owner attitude towards French culture and history. At home we enjoyed a somewhat furtive camaraderie that relished our shared fluency in French and sometimes resorted to it as a private intimate code for sharing subversive ideas. One of those was an aesthetic disgust with Pa's pronunciation of French. It came quite close at times to a caricature of the Englishman's accent that we used to parody *entre nous* and with our Lycee playmates as a shameful dialect that we would at all costs avoid – symptomatic of ignorance, and arrogant jingoism. We did not suspect Pa of nationalistic chauvinism, knowing him to be a strong advocate of European culture grounded in a deep knowledge of French and German history and literature. But we found it fun, behind his back, to ridicule his inability to steer clear of the connotations of jingoism inherent in the prototypical English accent when speaking French.

My father's perspective on my emerging bilingualism included admiration and a touch of anxiety, revealed to me in an incident that has stayed with me over the years as a kind of epiphany.

> Pa was, I suppose, dimly aware of his children's standing joke at his expense, since he evoked it indirectly one day at home when he took me to task for what he perceived as an analogous mispronunciation of English. 'I am proud of the way you are able to speak French with a French accent,' he said, 'but let me never hear you speaking English with a French accent.' I don't recollect how conscious I had been of doing so. Possibly I had been joking, deliberately parodying the pronunciation of English by some of my francophone playmates

or teachers. But the reprimand struck me at the time as both unwarranted in its moralistic overtone and symptomatic of a degree of ethnolinguistic narrowness that was unworthy of his generally inclusive liberalism.

Music and Visual Arts

Some of the intellectually focused activities in my Barnes family life were deliberately organised as learning opportunities. Some, such as board games and hobbies, were pleasurable, others less so. My hobbies included collecting various items: matchboxes, beer mats, postage stamps, coins, toy knights in armour. Organising those collections afforded an early introduction to taxonomy. A more sustained hobby that I was introduced to in childhood was photography. Although the techniques of developing and printing in the dark room have since been rendered obsolete by digital technology, I still derive great pleasure from composing photographs on my cell phone camera and sharing them with correspondents.

Learning to play a musical instrument was regarded as a requirement, and I was routinely reminded to 'do my practice' on the violin for a stipulated period of time before being allowed to go out and play. I attended violin lessons once a week, but never made much progress. Despite my poor performance on the violin, appreciating music became a very pleasurable aspect of my childhood. Every Christmas, we would attend carol concerts, and I enjoyed singing carols, with minimal attention to the meaning of the lyrics, long before I became aware in adolescence of pop songs. In the sitting room a conspicuous item of furniture was the old-fashioned gramophone with a huge, horn-shaped loudspeaker, on which Mummy would sometimes play vinyl records for us. One of her favourites was a collection of spiritual and folk songs performed by the famous bass-baritone singer, Paul Robeson, including *Ol' Man River* and *Sometimes I feel like a motherless child*. I was deeply impressed by Robeson's magnificent voice, and relished the passionate modulation of his singing. But I do not recall associating the emotion with the injustices reflected in the lyrics, let alone with the political oppression of his people against which Robeson became famous for his protests. Indeed, when I learned as an adult about his political activism, it came as a surprise. At some point, I attended along with Hicky several of the Robert Mayer Children's Concerts at the Festival Hall in Central London. These introduced me to the idea of following an orchestral piece on the written score, which I later carried with me on outings to the promenade concerts held at the Royal Albert Concert Hall. I developed a preference quite early in life for orchestral compositions of the Romantic period of Western music by Beethoven, Brahms and Tchaikowski.

Appreciation of the visual arts was also presented to me mainly as a spectator sport, although I recall sometimes sitting side-by-side with Pa while each of us made a drawing of scenery using coloured crayons, and his commenting on the quality of my picture. I grew up feeling that art was a legitimate and enjoyable medium of self-expression, but one in which my aptitude was unremarkable, like my performance of music, and I rated it a less worthwhile domain for exploring than the domains of verbal expression in speech and writing.

Literacy as a Source of Entertainment

Solitary reading was an activity as commonplace in my childhood as taking physical exercise, and was accorded greater priority in the family's intimate culture than playing sports. From an early age I had my own borrower's card at the local library, where I would pick out, with guidance from the librarian, novels aimed at my age group. Later a favourite pastime became browsing the family *Chambers's Encyclopaedia* in search of knowledge about esoteric aspects of the real world that captured my imagination, including archaeology and the history of writing. I don't recall ever being told that I was not mature enough to read about certain topics, except for a mild admonition from my mother when she found me reading the text of *King Lear* in my pre-adolescent years. She advised me that I might do well to postpone reading that particular treasured work of Shakespeare until I had lived a bit longer. She offered the same advice about *Othello*. This was a rare departure from her general encouragement to read whatever caught my interest. As a result of that permissiveness, I think I may have missed the full impact of some adult literature later in life by being exposed to it before I was developmentally ready to understand it.

Engagement with the performing art of drama was cultivated in an informal way in my early childhood, with an unsupervised game of 'dressing-up'. A large box of old clothes was dedicated to the activity, which sometimes gave rise to little plays put on for an audience of parents. Watching live theatre was a rare and special treat, sometimes at The Old Vic in central London. I was impressed and somewhat envious when my best friend at the Lycee, David La Bouchardiere was cast at the age of eleven in a pantomime staged at a West End theatre.

The Neighbourhood

Our house was located in Barnes, a middle-class residential suburb on the South-West side of London, from which many people commuted to work in the city. It was a relatively affluent section of post-War London society and I took it for granted that every family, like ours, had enough food to ensure adequate nutrition.

The houses all had regular supplies of electricity, treated water and sanitation, and land-line telephone connections. When I was considered old enough, I was given a bicycle as a birthday present, and this gave me access to a wider range of territory for exploration, including riding to the location of my scout troupe meetings. Our family used public transport to travel into the city. As the double-deckered bus crossed over the river Thames from Barnes to Hammersmith, it felt like venturing from a quiet safe home territory into the hectic world of the city. Alighting from the bus, we crossed a busy traffic intersection on foot and entered the Tube station. During rush hour, the station was teeming with hurrying passengers on their way to or from the platforms where we would board a train to South Kensington, the nearest stop to our school, the Lycee.

The family moved to Barnes in 1951, the year I turned seven, leaving behind a block of flats in Earls Court. The move was celebrated by my father as a step up in the world: instead of living in a rented flat, he was now a homeowner and rate payer. I recall him on one occasion speculating aloud about the social characteristics of other residents of Barnes. They included a few public figures such as film actors and TV producers, and a news item about one of them had triggered the conversation. I remember being intrigued, as I listened, by his seemingly ambivalent sense of ownership and belonging, touched with under-tones of irony. We were, he acknowledged, insiders to the local community. But, at the same time, he affirmed a certain independence from its implicit norms. We lived *in* suburbia, but we were *not defined by* it in a way that many of our neighbours were, and he was proud of being able to rise above its parochial small-mindedness. The only other family resident in Barnes that I recall us knowing at all well was the Hankeys. Uncle Richard was one of Pa's best friends since college, working as a solicitor. He lived a short walk from our house, with his wife and son. He was one of my godfathers, a very gentle and approachable man who taught me to play chess and treated me as a virtual member of his family (see Figure 3).

Citizen of the World

From an early age, I was encouraged to think of myself as a citizen of the world. A silent declaration of our family's sociocultural situation beyond the confines of the neighbourhood was the wall-papering of the stairwell of our house with maps of various geographical zones such as North America, Western Europe, the Middle East, and Africa. These were pasted side-by-side all over the walls of the passageway. Sometimes Hicky and I would test one another with questions about where a particular geographical feature was located relative to another: 'which river runs closest to <a particular city>'. The background to this quizzing was one of Pa's favourite family games, in which he would set up a competition between us about general knowledge. In order to compete successfully, we memorised the capital city of each nation and other such global information trivia.

Another way in which our childhood was geared to instilling a sense of global citizenship was the practice of going on holiday to Europe. On two occasions we went *en famille* to France, once to stay in a Paris apartment while the French owners, friends of our parents, were out of town, the other time to stay in a rented cottage in a village in Brittany. When I was nine, I was sent on my own to stay with a German family. My hosts were Jewish refugees from Nazi Germany who had made friends with my parents in London during the War. They now lived in a city flat with their two sons and a baby daughter. I had never met them before and did not take a liking to the boys.

> One day, I was alone in the flat with their housekeeper, whom I was shadowing as she went about her daily chores. We were standing in front of the bathroom washbasin when she said something to the effect that her boss was 'a dirty man,' the ostensible evidence being his habit of not rinsing the washbasin after shaving. I derived two prescriptive messages from this: one practical 'When I grow old enough to shave, I should always rinse the basin after using it,' the other more general and moral 'I should think about the consequences of my actions for others and try to be considerate.'

Looking back with a more elaborate understanding of the sociocultural context, I realise now that my caregiver's moral judgment was probably influenced by a stereotype, actively promoted by Nazi propaganda and still prevalent in immediate post-war Germany, of Jews as culturally deficient and antisocial. But my ignorance of the wider societal context deprived me of understanding that.

Introduction to Violence

The intimate culture of our family at home was virtually devoid of violence. Earlier in our lives, my sister, Hicky, and I recall seeing a hairbrush ominously displayed as a warning that, should we exhaust our mother's patience, the ultimate sanction would be a paddling with it on our backsides. But neither of us recalls the actual experience of being beaten: it was alluded to as something no longer suitable after a certain age. Toy soldiers were part of my parentally framed play repertoire, and sometimes a playmate and I would take sides and organise opposing armies into pitched battles. Of course, there was no blood shed in these clashes, and we tried not to make them so violent as to damage the toys. One of our family's notorious story themes over the years was that my sister, Hicky, and I were forever fighting. But neither of us, in old age, recalls the experience of fear or pain from those recurrent conflicts. What we both remember vividly is that parental intervention took the form of separating us: we were sent off to our respective bedrooms and forbidden to continue the quarrel.

Our home was a cloistered world in which we children were protected against the immediate spectacle of real violence. Our expeditions into wider society were closely regulated. Apart from attending school and visiting the homes of our parents' friends, there was the local Wolf Cubs pack in which I was enrolled, graduating after a certain age into the Sea Scouts. The cubs and scouts felt like an alien tribe, where children spoke with a different accent from the one we used at home. The culture of the Cubs was gentle and warm, but that of the Sea Scouts to which I graduated around the age of eleven was much rougher. On one occasion, I witnessed conspicuous violence imposed by a senior scout on a boy of my age as punishment for excessive swearing. The offender was pinned by his peers against a tree while the older boy poured antiseptic into his mouth. He screamed with pain, and I just watched in dismay. My feeling of revulsion was followed with shame at not having intervened to protest. I did not report the incident to my parents.

At one point, my parents decided I needed to learn how to defend myself physically. I suspect that at some level of consciousness my father considered it a part of preparing me for manhood. He chose as my instructor one of his best friends, known to us as Uncle Bill – a huge man whom I loved and respected. Bill was assigned the task of teaching me how to box. His credentials for taking on this assignment included his status as a war hero, having survived internment in a Japanese camp in Singapore. He went about it in a jovial way, sparring with me in boxing gloves purchased for that express purpose. Soon I was told I was ready to join the boxing club at school as part of my assigned recreational activity programme. I felt a bit uneasy about this, but went along with it for a while.

> One day I was matched with a boy I knew only slightly. Putting into effect my newly acquired skills, I led the attack with my left fist and, when an opening appeared, followed through with a strong right punch to my opponent's head. And suddenly I saw that his nose was bleeding profusely. The 'fight' was stopped, and all the people in the gym crowded round him in caring sympathy. There was a lot of blood, and I was overwhelmed with guilt.

From that day forward I declared to myself, and to my parents, that I would never again participate in the heinous sport of boxing. I have no recollection of resistance by the parental unit, or of pressure to change my mind. It was just accepted that Robbie does not like boxing, does not watch boxing matches, and certainly doesn't box himself.

My later life journey took me to many other places and gave rise to other networks of people with whom I developed a sense of belonging, including friendships, collaborations, and a next generation of families.

3 Adolescent Challenges at Boarding School (London 1957–1961)

Westminster School

My entry into Westminster was an intensively prepared transition. Both of my parents had attended single-sex, independent secondary schools and they held the principle of privately funded education in high regard. Westminster was ranked among England's top so-called 'public schools' alongside Eton, with a record of successfully grooming their students for entry into the elite universities of Oxford and Cambridge. For boys without special family connections, the standard route of access was a competitive academic exam for the award of scholarships to about eight candidates per year. I received preparation for the exam for about a year at Davies's (a private tutorial college in central London), including my first exposure to classical Greek.

I was enrolled as a weekly boarder which effectively insulated me from the rest of my family of origin, my sister having enrolled at a different boarding school for girls, and my parents moving soon afterwards to Singapore where my father was attached to the British High Commission as a senior security official. Westminster school was a very different niche from our family home in Barnes – larger, more socially prestigious, highly structured and supportive intellectually, but lacking in coherent guidance for my socioemotional development, which as an adolescent I was expected to manage myself Beyond its reputation for educational excellence, the school was exciting for me personally in several ways: its historic architecture, its encouragement of private study, and, most of all, the individual attention that some of the teachers accorded to our interests and needs in class. However, unlike most of my peers, this was my first experience of single-gender education, and I regarded that as anomalous compared with the co-educational policy of the Lycee. I was uneasy with what I perceived as the community's normative approval of homosexual relations between older and younger boys, and suspicious of the established practice of delegating authority to monitors who were just a year or two older than those of us in their charge.

The architectural setting of the school was extraordinary, adjacent to the great Abbey, where English monarchs had been crowned since 1066. Every evening we entered the Abbey via the Cloisters, which abutted onto the School Yard, and proceeded inside to St Faith's Chapel for prayers. I recall being deeply moved by the huge Gothic arches above our heads, and the powerful resonance of organ music that was often played by someone rehearsing at that time of day. Across the Square from the Abbey were the Houses of Parliament, and the chimes of the clock, Big Ben, resounded every quarter in our classrooms and our dormitory throughout the day and night. The school's own premises were located around Little Dean's Yard, including Ashburnham House, inside which a magnificent oak staircase swept in a broad curve up to the library on the second floor. The boys selected for the award of scholarships were known as Queen's Scholars and housed in a separate residence called College. Pa found this institution steeped in history thrilling, and shared his enthusiasm with me by plying me with antique volumes about the Abbey's architecture and monuments, which remain in my personal library to this day.

Academic instruction was delivered in small classes of less than twenty students, combining scholars with other boys accommodated in the different houses of the school. But College afforded a uniquely conducive environment for working on class assignments ('prep') and independent study. The intimate culture of College included respect for silent reading, for which time was dedicated every weekday in addition to the ninety minutes reserved for prep.

Deep Friendships, Romantic Fantasies

Overnight accommodation in College was provided in the form of a shared dormitory for each cohort of students, and within that setting our cohort developed its own intimate culture, incorporating some aspects of the larger meaning systems of College and Westminster, but also forging some deviant themes. The small group of seven of us who entered College in 1957 became a peer group, within which there were frequent opportunities to bond. The beds in our dorm were spaced several feet apart, and we were required to be silent a short while after 'lights out'. Thereafter, holding a conversation that would not be detected by a monitor patrolling the corridor required moving into close proximity and whispering. One of my two closest friendships was established in that way. Simon Mollison and I took turns to sit on the window-sill next to the other's bed, sharing ideas and anecdotes late into the night (see Figure 2). My other closest friend was Eric Arnold, with whom I shared a hobby interest in archaeology that fuelled long daytime conversations about Egyptian hieroglyphics, and on one occasion an expedition together to visit in Bloomsbury the obscure Flinders Petrie Museum. Those friendships were not exclusive, and I recall many fruitful conversations with other boys in our dorm and beyond. But the bonds I formed with Eric and Simon remained an important source of emotional support throughout our adolescence and into early adulthood when we were at university, generating

Figure 2 Robert with close friends Eric and Simon – Westminster
School photo 1958.

a unique level of trust that persisted across our adult lives despite wide geographical separation, such that, when we got married, even our respective spouses
learned to respect our need for one-on-one time together whenever we visited one
another's homes.

It is surely no coincidence that those first profound friendships emerged at
a juncture in my life-journey when the parents and sibling who supported me
through my childhood in Barnes were no longer so accessible due to our
geographical separation. Two other friendships rivalled them in intensity in
my early adulthood: with Chris Russell and with Mansur Lalljee (see Section 4).
Over the years at Westminster, I learned to regard homosexual affections
between boys as understandable, and, under the influence of Oscar Wilde's
writings, I came to endorse the principle of consensual sexual orientation as
a basic human right. A movement towards decriminalisation of homosexuality
between consenting adults gathered momentum in England during this period,
notably with the publication of the Wolfenden Committee (1957) report.
However, I never personally engaged in homosexual practices, finding the
very idea sensually dissonant.

Like most adolescent boys, with the advent of puberty I experienced a new
kind of interest in girls, but my opportunities to explore them were severely
restricted by Westminster's single-gender policy, and they remained almost
entirely in the realm of fantasy. For a few months in 1959 I fancied myself in
love with a girl called Vanessa, with whom I had danced at a party. For a while
I felt guilty whenever I was attracted to other girls, but after a few months
I realised that we were not intellectually compatible, and backed off. In an entry
in my personal diary, I reflected that my 'love affair' with Vanessa was over and

that I was fortunate that despite its intensity, the ending of my 'little passion' had not caused me deep distress. The entry, which was in French, continued:

> I am trying to make a new start: I need friends – not just a few personal friends. I would like to have a bit of charm to win me friendship all around. I think I have developed enough of a personality in my own eyes. It's now overdue to try and make myself understood by others, to mankind, to people I have known, perhaps to myself. I have studied others. It's time to make a little effort to present myself to that community in whose thoughts I am so interested . . . I need to try really hard . . . to give, instead of always seeking to receive what interests and pleases me.

It seems this was a turning point in my personal outlook, centering on the importance of giving and communicating with others. I felt highly self-critical of my early forays into relationships with girls, dismissing as delusional, almost as soon as it started, my first explicit infatuation with Vanessa. I was surrounded by age-mates who thought they might be falling into homosexual love with an older boy at school, and I gave serious consideration to that possibility myself. But my sensual intuitions pointed elsewhere, and I kept hoping that one day I would find in real life the exhilarating emotions of romantic love with a woman who reciprocated my admiration and loyalty. That was an ideal celebrated in the poetry and drama of classical Greek and Latin literature, and in nineteenth-century English and French novels and poetry.

Aesthetic Appreciation

My childhood socialisation had instilled an ethical orientation that valued pleasure in the arts above material goods. Much of my mental energy in adolescence was invested in the spiritual adventure of developing my own personal taste.

The architecture and sculptures in Westminster Abbey afforded many opportunities for the development of aesthetic appreciation in the domain of visual art. Drawing on my father's earlier tutoring, I explored the harmonious contrast between the graceful gothic arches of the cathedral's thirteenth century nave and transept and the magnificent fan vault ceiling of the sixteenth-century Henry VIIth Chapel and the eighteenth-century Hawksmoor towers. I savoured the solemnity of the effigies of King Edward I and Eleanor of Castile, and scorned the flashy marble decor of many of the monuments in Poet's Corner, as frivolously unworthy of the great minds they sought to honour, such as Keats. Within walking distance from school for a weekend outing was the Tate Gallery – where I delighted in the seascapes and sunsets of Turner, the French impressionist paintings by Monet and Degas, and Picasso's blue period.

In my adolescent engagement with music, I focused heavily on the sensual dimension of representation. My closest friends and I used to dance vigorously to classical music played on our gramophones, in ways that derived not from the regular cultural themes of the music, but from our enthusiasm. Even now, when I listen to recordings of Beethoven symphonies and concertos, I am tempted to move my arms in time with the rhythms of the music, as though I were conducting the orchestra. But my aesthetic delight in listening to music was not matched with committed engagement in its performance on my chosen instrument, the violin. By the time I reached Westminster at age thirteen, I was competent enough to play in an orchestra, but was aware that my talent was very limited. My violin teacher, Miss Ireland, was strict about position, insisting that I hold the violin in a particular way, which I found painful and increasingly deemed unnecessary. Having learned to read sheet music, I started to try my hand at sight-reading various classical Sonatas and Concertos, delighting in a few sequences that I was able to master. But when I showed off my accomplishment to my teacher she gave me a severe lecture, insisting that without observing the strict discipline she was trying to instill in me I would never achieve excellence. I rudely declared that excellence was clearly unattainable for me due to my limited talent and was not my goal, but that I would like to enjoy the music I could play. She considered this an ignoble attitude and soon afterwards we parted company. I suppose the authorities at school reported it as 'dropping out' of an optional extra feature of the curriculum.

I learned a bit about performing arts in three other contexts: choral singing, recitation, and drama. A unique tradition at Westminster was The Latin Play, performed in front of an invited audience, and one year I was cast as Syrus, the slave, in an outdoor production of Terence's play *Adelphi* in Little Dean's Yard, directed by our widely acclaimed Classics teacher, Theo Zinn. In my last term at Westminster, our English teacher Stephen Lushington put on a production of Shakespeare's *King Lear.* I was excited and auditioned for the title role, but was disappointed to learn that I been assigned the peripheral part of Cornwall.

Theo Zinn's pedagogical method sought to engage us with the cultures of ancient Greece and Rome in multiple ways. The authors whose texts he assigned us to study in the original languages included playwrights, poets, and historians. Beyond translation of their texts into English, he invited us to interpret their philosophical ideas, and led us in open-ended class discussions that blended linguistic etymology and political history with epistemology and ethics (although I only discovered those disciplinary terms at university). One strand of this wide-ranging curriculum was reading aloud Greek and Latin poetry with feeling, an exercise in rhetorical skill. I still retain as part of my personal intellectual inventory a memorised speech by Hector on the battlefield of the siege of Troy in Homer's *Iliad*. Over and above the regular classics curriculum, Theo earned my profound respect for the breadth and depth of the topics on which he cultivated our engagement, ranging from nurturing our aesthetic appreciation of Beethoven's late quartets to reflection on the connections and contrasts between the elite cultures of Athens and Rome. His deployment of the Socratic method of questioning left a lasting impression in my intellectual repertoire. My practice as a supervisor of graduate research has been to begin with probing questions to the student about what she or he already knows, leading her in steps towards a deeper understanding of herself and of the domain of inquiry that we are exploring together. And our research team's exploration of parental ethnotheories in Baltimore followed a similar approach (see Section 7).

Introspective Examination of Religious Faith

Institutionalised religion came into focus for me in adolescence. As a child, I had occasionally attended Sunday School at the local Church of England church, but I had celebrated Easter and Christmas holidays more as occasions for eating special foods, exchanging gifts, and decorating the house than for reflecting on spiritual or moral issues. At Westminster, I was obliged as a Queen's Scholar to participate in ritualised group worship on Sunday mornings, dressed in a black gown and a white shirt with butterfly collar and white bowtie, joining the procession of the choir and sitting with them in the great Abbey. There we recited prayers, listened to Bible readings and sang hymns. More significant for me were the low-key evening services in a side-chapel (St Faith's). There, in the dim lighting, I was allowed to stay on after the short Plainsong for private, silent meditation. On a less regular schedule, informal seminars were held in the College Master's premises, at which writings by modern Christian apologetic authors such as G. K. Chesterton and C. S. Lewis were discussed.

My personal diaries for those years include a number of allusions to soul-searching about my emerging beliefs. In March 1959, two months before I turned fifteen, I wrote, following a long spell of meditation in St Faith's Chapel:

> I became extremely enthusiastic about this idea of a general, basic religion: the Deity . . . instituted all religions. Discrepancies among them are explicable by different interpretations of the same essential truth. I went through the Abbey with that deliciously exhilarating sensation I occasionally experience of being convinced that I have solved for myself the whole problem of life (or am on the way to doing so).

My notes drift between philosophy and literature, and centre on the need for 'a clear-cut method for deciding. . . in matters where two moral duties appear to be conflicting'. My sense now, looking back, is that I shelved the philosophical puzzle of how to deal with moral conflicts until my final year of studies at Oxford, relying in the interim on the notion of being an agnostic to excuse myself from taking a definitive position. However, 'keeping an open mind' is not necessarily a symptom of evasiveness. It may be an honest way of express- ing not just that I don't know, but also a tentative declaration that knowing for sure in that domain is logically impossible, at least for me as I currently understand myself.

Interpersonal Violence

Rough and tumble play occurred occasionally at Westminster in the playground, the gym or the dormitory. But it was generally frowned upon and I avoided contact sports, where it was no doubt encouraged. The officially sanctioned practice of disciplinary caning struck me as anomalous, especially when it was administered by monitors. An instructive example was the case in which a boy was so enraged by the brutality of his caning that he returned to the monitor's room where it had been administered to ravage his tormentor's personal belong- ings. The monitor was moved to call the violent protester back later and present his contrite apologies, claiming that he hadn't realised his own strength. He was known to my peer group as a gentle, quiet person and his courage in apologising to his victim earned our respect. We pledged to one another that in future when we became eligible for the authority as monitors to administer corporal punish- ment, we would never exercise it.

In my third year, I had a crucial encounter with violence, administered by the head of the institution, which radically impacted my overall attitude towards Westminster. Two boys with a history of getting up to mischief had been informed at their latest disciplinary hearing that they would not be caned or expelled, but warned that this was their last chance. A group of their friends decided this was a cause for celebration. So, at the weekend, we assembled in a corner of the school undergoing renovation, with a freshly purchased supply of forbidden substances: beer, wine, and cigarettes. We were having a good time and probably making too much noise, when we were discovered by a school prefect. The five of us were reported for the offence of 'drinking and smoking in school', and soon afterwards we were informed that we should report to the Headmaster's residence, one at a time, starting with the youngest two and ending with the two original offenders, Simon and Anthony.

The Headmaster, Mr Carleton, was a large man in his fifties, known for addiction to his pipe, and nicknamed Coot. He was notorious both for harsh caning and for unwelcome petting advances on boys referred to him for disciplinary action. We prepared ourselves by soaking our buttocks in cold water to buffer the pain and donning our thickest underpants in case we were allowed to keep them on. Each of the first two victims returned from their beating after a few minutes to report to the group. I don't recall any tears. When it was my turn, I received a slightly larger number of strokes than the two who preceded me. But, like them, I was relieved that I was not required to undress before bending over. It was all over in a matter of minutes, and very few words were exchanged. The strokes were definitely painful, but not enough to make me cry out, and I felt I was able to maintain some dignity as I walked out of the torture chamber of Coot's plush sitting room.

Simon and Anthony's sessions were significantly longer than ours, thirty to forty-five minutes each. Both of them were required to undress before caning, and the consequential injuries sustained by Simon were what shocked me the most. I was horrified by the sight of the bleeding weals across his buttocks, and felt the least I could do was to assist him to access some palliative treatment, while also drawing the severity of his injuries to the attention of a responsible adult. So, the next morning, when Simon woke up feeling very sore, I escorted him to Matron's clinic, which was situated not far from our dormitory at the top of a narrow flight of stairs. One of the duties of the Matron was to pronounce as an authority on the significance of illnesses or injuries incurred by boys in residence, to prescribe appropriate remedial treatment and if need be to provide a note to excuse the boy from normal school activities (known as an 'L.O.').

> I recall vividly the dramatic configuration: the two of us boys huddled at the foot of the staircase looking up, and Matron standing in the doorway of her clinic looking down at us. Simon was playing up his inability to walk without assistance as a ploy to ensure that our report would be taken seriously. He was leaning against me with his arm around my shoulders for support. She sternly asked what was our business, and I reported that Simon had been caned by the Headmaster last night, and his injuries were so bad that this morning he was hardly able to walk. So he needed an LO. She firmly replied that we should go away, without asking to inspect the injuries, or offering any palliative treatment.

I was astonished and outraged. Here was an adult whom I had respected as a professional supporter of our physical well-being, *in loco parentis*, deliberately refusing to examine a schoolboy's injuries, let alone consider the possibility of recommending him for exemption from school activities. I realised, as I reflected on the event, that she was morally compromised by her commitment to respecting the Headmaster's right to cane boys savagely, and that she placed higher priority on adherence to the school's code of authority than on protection of the physical and emotional well-being of the adolescents under her professional care.

In correspondence some fifty years later, Simon recollected the impact of his caning quite differently:

> there was a question of expulsion for Anthony and me and that would have meant the collapse of my world. It was this threat, not the pain and humiliation of being caned, that made me resolve to try and stay out of trouble in future. Although it was a savage beating, I don't recall being traumatised by it.

My own reaction, after a brief spell of indulgence in self-pity for the immediate pain, was to focus on the injustice represented by the brutality, which had inflicted significant physical injury on my friend.

An opportunity arose several months later to strike back in a covert way. Rumour had it that another schoolboy, Miller (a pseudonym), was scheduled for a caning by the Headmaster, as punishment for some minor offence. My friend Chris and I decided on a form of direct action to prevent repetition of the savage punishment inflicted on Simon and Anthony. Slipping out of school at the appointed hour, we phoned Coot's office from a public call box, and, putting on a disguised voice, I introduced myself as the news editor of a tabloid newspaper renowned for its sensational *exposes* of scandals. Affecting what I thought would be the manner of such a publication's editor, I told him that we understood he was planning to cane one of the boys in his charge, and warned that if he were to proceed with doing so, we would print on the front page of our paper tomorrow an account of his shocking abuse of power. We were gratified to learn through the grapevine that Miller (from whom we had kept our ploy a secret) reported to his friends that Coot had received a phone call while he was already in the office awaiting his punishment. Putting down the phone, Coot had asked Miller if he knew anything about the call, and then promptly dismissed him.

When I was informed a year or two later that I was a candidate for appointment as Head Boy and encouraged, with that as an incentive, to stay on, after sitting the university entrance exams, I recollected the Coot-Matron alliance, as well as the older boy's outburst of violence on one of the junior boys when he was a monitor. These were evidence for me of an evil system I was being invited to join as a subaltern authority figure. I realised that any attempt on my part in such a role to stand up to or mitigate the punitive system in place would quickly be overruled, and I declined. I later wrote to the Head of College to explain, but never received a reply.

Planning an Escape

My class with Theo Zinn that year was a combination of two cohorts, known as the VIIth. I sought permission and was allowed to sit for the exam a year earlier than usual. I crammed together with an agemate in the senior stream, and when the results came out, we were each awarded a classics scholarship at Corpus Christi. We were also both advised to wait a year before coming up, as we were considered too young to benefit fully from life at university. When I received notice of the award, I ran out of the school grounds, across the road onto a favourite spot near Parliament beside Rodin's sculpture of the Burgers of Calais, and rolled in the grass, celebrating my pass to freedom. I wrote to my parents in Singapore seeking their consent to leave school, and arrogantly declaring that I had now acquired the skills needed to direct my own pursuit of knowledge without expert guidance and supervision.

4 Learning to Assume Responsibility: Emerging Adulthood (Singapore 1961–1962, Oxford 1962–1965)

In this section, I describe how my participation in the student life of the University of Singapore triggered a growth of political consciousness that later informed my political activism as an undergraduate in Oxford. Engagement with the struggle against racism in my personal life converged with an academic introduction to philosophy as a discipline to inform some exploratory public participation in politics under the aegis of the student club called the Joint Action Committee Against Racial Intolerance (JACARI) and my decision to apply for the position of research fellow at the University of Zambia, sowing the initial seeds of my later explicit dissent with Western cultural hegemony. Arriving in Singapore at the age of seventeen, I was admitted to the university as an occasional student and was enchanted by the inclusive welcome I received in a society with a vastly different culture and history from the European niche in which I had been raised. Inspired with an infectious enthusiasm for multi-ethnic camaraderie, I plunged into the social life of the campus. I fell in love with a beautiful young woman, joyously courted her as a partner and, when our romance was interrupted, made a commitment of loyalty to our union. At Oxford University, I divided my energies between formal studies of psychology and philosophy and extracurricular activism focusing on how to challenge the injustices of racial discrimination and oppression.

Exploring Adulthood in Singapore (1961–1962)

As I left school in 1961, my life-purpose was to focus my energy on self-expression through writing poetry. With some gentle persuasion from my admired Uncle Bill whom I visited in Geneva, I agreed, instead of trying to live independently in Paris, to accept my parents' invitation to stay in their house in Singapore. They had negotiated on my behalf a position at the University of Singapore as a 'non-graduating student' entitled to attend classes across a wide range of subjects without submitting any written assignments or sitting for exams. On campus, I gravitated towards the English Department, hoping to find encouragement and support for my chosen agenda of creative writing, while also learning about life and literature from studying poetry and novels by English authors such as Keats, Hardy, Lawrence, and Forster. Concurrently, I dabbled eclectically in many different pools of intellectual activity, including Chinese calligraphy and anti-colonial politics. It soon became apparent that commuting from my parents' suburban compound to campus was depriving me of some of the most exciting student social life, and my parents agreed for me to move into a residence on campus. One evening, at a student-sponsored dinner dance at a restaurant off campus, I met Esther Jesudason, a recent graduate of a local Teacher Training College. I was struck by her beauty and charm and we set a date to meet again. The relationship grew in leaps and bounds, and we soon became lovers, spending many days and some nights together, mixing with a fun-loving, multiracial community of young adults.

Esther was the third of seven children born to Edward Jesudason, a Singaporean citizen of Tamil heritage in his first marriage with a woman of Chinese heritage. Esther's facial features displayed her mixed ethnic heritage in a uniquely beautiful blend. Our peer group included people with every shade of skin colour from the chocolate complexion of her father to the olive complexion of her mother and the parchment complexion of my parents. We attended many parties, dancing vigorously to rock-and-roll music, cruised around the city on her Vespa scooter, and often ended our evening with a late snack cooked on the streetside (*satay, pau,* or *pisang goreng*). English was our shared language and that of our respective families, but she taught me the elements of the city's *lingua franca,* known as Bazaar Malay, which became part of our intimate dialect. By the time I met her, Esther was living with several siblings at her father's home and his second wife, Poh Chan, together with several young children from the second marriage. Most of them accepted me as Esther's boyfriend and I became a frequent visitor at their home, often playing with her younger siblings.

However, Esther's elder brother Eddie took exception to our relationship, suspecting that I would abandon his sister, possibly making her pregnant, and return to England leaving her in disgrace. One day, when the affair had been going strong for several months, Eddie confronted me at the doorway of the house, forbade me to continue seeing Esther, and challenged me to a boxing duel. I was astonished and confused: it seemed he was unwilling to discuss the matter in a peaceful way, and I reluctantly gave in to the challenge to defend my honour with my fists. We set a time for the duel at a quiet spot on the edge of campus, and met there each accompanied by a second, and started to exchange blows without gloves. In between blows, I tried to reason with him, assuring him that his sister and I were in love, that my intentions were honourable, but that, as I had not yet reached the age of eighteen, I would need my parents' consent to get married, and was not yet sure of their support. He was surprised to learn my age, having assumed I was in my twenties like Esther, who had just turned twenty-one. By this time we were both quite tired and bruised, and with the approval of our seconds, we agreed to call the duel a draw. I think we even shook hands.

The next time, I went home, word had reached Pa through his colleagues in the local police that I had been observed in a fight. My black eye was still unmistakable, and I was forced to explain what had happened. This entailed revealing my relationship with Esther, which I had hitherto kept secret from my parents. My motivation for the secrecy was a mixture of adolescent determination to preserve my independence and a creeping awareness that my father was less open-minded than I had believed him to be when growing up in England.

During my earlier visits to Singapore for my summer holidays from Westminster, I had felt some discomfort with the colonial lifestyle of the family home in a segregated suburban compound reserved for British diplomats, where the only indigenous residents were domestic servants. But I had 'gone with the flow' of expatriate social life, even dating some of the daughters of my father's British work colleagues. Now, as a student on the multi-racial university campus, it dawned on me as a shock that my friends would not be admitted at the Singapore Swimming Club, which enforced a colour bar. It was Pa's favourite resort for getting the exercise he much needed given his office job. When I challenged him about it, Pa pointed out that it was the biggest pool in the city, and that another big pool was similarly reserved for only Chinese patrons. I countered that two wrongs don't make a right, and that racial discrimination was an abhorrent social practice, contrary to the fundamental principles of egalitarian democracy. The next time he invited me to join him there for a swim, I declined. My mother then decided to take out membership of the Island Club, which had a smaller pool, but an open-door policy for all races, and we frequented it together on a number of occasions. Mummy never openly stated her disapproval of Pa's compliance with racial discrimination at the swimming club, and I took this as a sign that she felt bound by marital loyalty to keep her head down. However, her more progressive perspective on race relations was manifest in other ways, such as her part-time job at Nanyang University, where she was the only non-Chinese lecturer.

At the time of the fight with Eddie, early in 1962, I had given little thought to the question of my parents' racial attitudes, sensing just that they operated in a different world from me. So I was ill-prepared for the position taken by Pa in his formal confrontation with me.

It had been decided, he informed me, that I should leave Singapore forthwith and wait out in England the remaining months before 'going up' to Oxford. I indignantly demanded an explanation, and the words in which it was delivered cut deep into my heart. 'You are too young', my father said, 'to get involved with a woman who is older than you and of another race'. I protested strongly, affirming that I knew what I was doing, and he had no business interfering in my love affair, to which he replied that I was under age and obliged to accept his ruling. 'And if I refuse, what are you going to do about it?' I retorted. 'Are you going to fight me?' I asked, puffing out my chest.

But I didn't push that idea, sensing that violence had already proven to be a poor way of resolving disagreement with Eddie. I went to meet Esther and we discussed various alternative courses of action. One would be for us to elope, perhaps to North Borneo, where she would not need a passport as a citizen of Malaysia. But eventually we decided that our options would be broader in England, and that I should comply for the moment, while she made plans to join me there.

Engagement against the Odds

By way of mitigation for the indignity of this forced repatriation, I was offered the option of traveling by passenger ocean liner instead of by plane, and I chose it as a way to buffer the pain of separation from Esther. The two-week journey was a dream-like experience. I spent most of the time on board reflecting on the interruption of my love-affair with Esther and writing her long letters about it. Our commitment to each other lasted throughout the months of waiting, and in due course she migrated as planned to England, where she found work as a kindergarten teacher and also spent time in London supporting her elder sister with caring for her new baby.

However, in 1964 Esther announced that she was no longer in love with me and demanded a break, prompting a deep emotional crisis for me that felt like the end of the world. I went on a solitary, week-long hiking trip in the Welsh mountains, during which I recorded in a personal diary a reflective search for explanation of what had gone wrong. I concluded that a key flaw had been my illusory assumption of total commonality between us:

> I have taken too much for granted and used you as if you were part of myself . . . as a lover I am too demanding, too impatient . . . I have treated you as I treat myself: with no respect, scarcely any compassion, and a determination to drive on to success . . . this is an unpardonable way to treat any other human being. To assume so much is to deny the other person's individuality . . . my desire now is for us both to live a life of reality, based on human responsibility. . . . My hope for our future . . . is that we may grow into two fuller individuals, enriched by a lasting and profound friendship . . . .

Wage Labour in London (1962)

On arrival in England, I resolved, as a matter of pride, not to draw on the bank account in which my parents had deposited funds for my maintenance. I rented a low-cost bed-sitter flat near Victoria Station and registered with an employment agency. I assured them that I was open to offers that required just manual labour skills, and was soon signed up for a temporary job as an office cleaner in the West End. From there I moved on to waiting tables at various small cafes, where I enjoyed the atmosphere and the left-over food I was allowed to take home after closing time, but not the massive dishwashing to which I was relegated on one occasion when the regular worker didn't show up. The cost of renting my home-base flat was shared with two former schoolfriends from Westminster. The first to join me there was Chris Russell, who had already explored the challenges of independently raising subsistence funds earlier in his life, by working as an unskilled labourer on building sites. Our friendship was grounded in our shared partnership in surreptitious defiance of authority at school and in shared feelings about distance from our respective lovers. Soon afterwards, our mutual friend Eric joined us in the flat, and the three of us developed an agreeable camaraderie. Later I found a better-paying part-time job conducting door-to-door market research interviews for an advertising agency, some of which I subcontracted to my flatmates. I opened a Post Office Savings bank account and set myself the goal of earning a surplus above my basic needs before the date for 'going up' to university. In September I proudly invested my savings of fifty pounds to purchase a reel-to-reel tape-recorder.

Student Life at Oxford (1962–1965)

My 'gap year' had led me to the conclusion that I no longer wanted to study English literature for which I felt inadequately talented, let alone Classical Latin and Greek which I had firmly rejected as insufficiently relevant to the modern world. Rather I would like to study psychology. It was a fairly ill-informed decision, and I wrote to inquire of the College to which I was admitted what I should read in preparation. I was advised to read an introductory text by Hebb (1949), titled *The Organization of Behavior*, which laid out in clear detail why the science of psychology had turned to the study of animal behaviour – a most unlikely avenue to understanding of the human soul, in the eyes of many humanities scholars. It was an excellent introduction to the culture of the Department of Experimental Psychology where I was assigned over my three years as an undergraduate to a series of animal behaviourist tutors (David Vowles, Stuart Sutherland, Nick Mackintosh). It even prepared me for the hostile attitude of the College President, W.F.R.Hardie, a classical scholar of philosophy in his sixties, who unsuccessfully tried his best to dissuade me from dropping Classics, and lost no opportunity to remind me of his scepticism whenever we met in the corridors of the College, exclaiming in his broad Scottish accent 'How are the rats, Mr Serpell?'

I bought in quite enthusiastically to the behaviourist paradigm (Broadbent, 1961), coupled with a search for neurophysiological correlates. My tutors, Sutherland and Mackintosh, convinced me that controlled experiments were a good way of testing theories, and that human behaviour shared certain regularities with other animal species, grounded in the structures and processes of our brains. Thus, cognition and learning could be studied productively by conducting experiments with rats or chickens in artificially restricted settings such as a laboratory maze. In my final year at Oxford, I had the opportunity to attend lectures by Niko Tinbergen who demonstrated the need to observe animals in their normal ecological context in order to understand their behaviour and adaptation. I largely ignored the topic of social psychology as presented by Michael Argyle due to extracurricular distractions, perhaps also dimly recognising and discouraged by the limitations criticised by Gustav Jahoda (1986) in publications I only encountered many decades later. But when I came across the early work of Henri Tajfel on social attitudes and prejudice, I approached him for a remedial course in preparation for the university's final examinations, thus beginning to build a connection between my academic studies and my political activism.

The only way to study psychology at Oxford in those days was as part of a double major in Psychology, with Philosophy or Physiology (PPP). Philosophy was a slightly less new field of study for me, having been introduced to Socrates by Theo at Westminster. But I was ill-prepared to appreciate the significance of Logic, on which the first two terms of the Oxford syllabus were focused. I was offended by the counter-intuitive absurdity of the logical rule that if the premise of a syllogism is false, then the syllogism is true, and saw no value in pursuing such anomalies. When I inquired about the possibility of switching my coursework from Philosophy to Physiology, I was advised that my grounding in the natural sciences was too weak to catch up. So I soldiered on with philosophy, and later came to enjoy it when I was exposed to university lectures by David Pears and others drawing on the tradition of Wittgenstein. My interest in philosophy was sustained by a new friendship, the most lasting one I formed at Oxford, with Mansur Lalljee. Our friendship included going for long walks along the riverside, where we shared our experiences with romantic love and an argumentative excitement about new ideas in philosophy and psychology, as well as drinking draught beer together in pubs, and eating curry. Mansur had come to Oxford with a BA degree from the University of Bombay, and entered the PPP programme in second year. His advance familiarity with many of the topics in philosophy combined with his lucid reasoning led me to regard him as a mentor.

The university's approach to monitoring the progress of student learning was very decentralised. Attendance at lectures was entirely optional, and the only focused assessment of my academic progress was left to my tutors, with whom I met once a week to present orally my essay on an assigned topic. The preparatory reading lists were generally insightfully composed, combining classic primary publications by distinguished authors with recent reports in mainstream academic journals, and at best the tutor's reaction to my essay was illuminating. But no grades were awarded, and it was only in my final year of studies that I learned informally from Dr Mackintosh that he expected me to be in the running for a First Class degree in the final university exams.

Outside of the prescribed curriculum, I pursued my interest in drama for a while, playing the lead parts in a French production at the Oxford Playhouse of Camus' *Caligula*, and in a college production of a 17th-century English play, *The Revenger's Tragedy*. I tried to apply Stanislavsky's acting principle of putting myself in the characters' shoes and performing as I personally would behave if I were in the character's situation. At best, I not only found the experience exhilarating, but also found it to be rather disturbing in the way it blurred the border between fantasy and reality. Like the art of rhetoric, I eventually concluded that stage-acting was a seductive avenue for self-expression that threatened to oversimplify and distort authentic participation in society. I went on in my subsequent professional career to favour accuracy over persuasiveness in the formulation of my thoughts for lectures and articles, and to avoid forming simplifying allegiances to social interest groups or political ideologies.

Political Activism

Looking back, I regard the most important of my learning experiences within Oxford University as my extracurricular activity in a student-run club called JACARI. Primed by my exposure to anti-colonial politics in Singapore and by my first-hand observations of racial prejudice in England, I was immediately drawn to the club's agenda, and became so actively involved in my second year that I neglected my academic obligations. The constitution of JACARI provided for representation on the executive committee from a broad range of political, religious, and cultural constituencies. As elected chair of the committee, I sought to broaden the group's mission beyond what was realistic for a band of young adults. In addition to inviting eminent speakers from around the world to address our meetings, we formed study groups to advocate for social change both in England and abroad, linking up with SNCC in the American civil rights movement and with the international anti-apartheid movement based in London. We even sent a delegation to lobby the British government to allocate more funds to the (then economically poor) Protectorate of Bechuanaland.

My role in that delegation resulted in my missing, on the same day, a demonstration in Oxford that drew attention in the press (Tuck, 2013). The focus of the event was an invited address to a conservative student group by the South African Ambassador. In our committee deliberations, some of us had advocated that we plant some critical voices in the audience to show up the hypocrisy of apartheid. But we were outvoted by some of my more radical peers, who argued that the talk should be pre-empted by picketing the building where it was advertised. Police were deployed to break up the demonstration and several students were arrested. My father, who generally kept his distance from my Oxford student career, phoned me from London in some alarm. I felt quite torn between assuring him that the demonstration had been held against my advice and wanting to affirm that the police should not have been deployed to protect a representative of the pernicious apartheid regime. It was my first taste of the challenging dilemma of deciding how to stand up for one's counter-establishment values against state intervention in the name of law and order.

Later that year JACARI took a more carefully prepared initiative to raise awareness of racism in English society. Many of our members were inter-national students, and some had experienced great difficulty in securing rented accommodation beyond what was available on college premises. In-house college rooms were too few to cater for more than a minority of the student body as a whole, and we suspected that the 'landladies' of other 'digs' were refusing to rent rooms to non-white students because of racial prejudice. JACARI conducted a survey in November 1964 after consultation with Dr Henri Tajfel, University Lecturer in Social Psychology. The findings were quite shocking by today's standards. Nearly 300 landlords or landladies were interviewed and a majority 'were found to exhibit clear signs of racial prejudice towards non-"white" students'. Specifically, '59 percent stated that they would hesitate to accept an application from an African or an Asian student even if all their rooms were free at the end of the summer vacation'. More than half of these 'were found to exhibit similar attitudes towards foreign students in general' (Serpell & Sneddon, 1965, pp. 332–333).

Although it was covered in the national press, I didn't follow up on the report, as I was no longer part of the leadership of JACARI, and was trying to keep my head down while catching up on studies for the imminent final exams. Nor did I pay attention to, if indeed I noticed, the backlash correspondence in the local

Figure 3 Rob (age 21) and Pa, with Uncle Richard (centre) looking on – London May 1965.

press, that Tuck (2013) described as follows: 'In angry letters to the proctors, Oxford's landladies defended the housing color bar', with a variety of specious arguments. Yet, re-reading our report several decades later, it seems that we leaned over backwards to first give reasoned consideration to the possibility that the negative attitudes expressed by many respondents were grounded in object-ively aversive experience with accommodating a student of colour, and then cited evidence to rebut that idea. Somewhat ahead of our time, we concluded that the right thing for the university authorities to do would be to refuse to include on a published list of approved accommodations for students any premises whose landlady was unwilling to give a categorical commitment to accept applicants irrespective of race. As Tuck (2013) reports in a sophisticated political analysis, the authorities predictably declined to follow our advice.

Plans for a New Life

After several months apart, in 1965, Esther and I re-engaged and decided that we were still in love. With only a few weeks to go, I decided to wait until my twenty-first birthday to inform my parents of our plan to marry. Meanwhile, my search for a job in which I might apply what I had learned at Oxford turned up an unexpected opportunity to combine my academic interests with my political orientation. A small advertisement appeared on the pin-board of the Psychology Department, inviting applications for a 3-year research fellowship at the newly established University of Zambia to study perception and learning in children. The position carried entitlement to local accommodation, international air fares and support for concurrent registration as a doctoral student at a university in the UK. In my application I cited, as evidence of academic qualification, my recently completed undergraduate research project on selective attention by young children at an Oxford kindergarten and, as evidence of moral commitment to post-colonial Zambia's national aspirations for progressive social change, my experience with JACARI and the anti-apartheid movement. I received an offer of appointment, following an interview in London, soon after receiving my graduation results and registration of my marriage with Esther. My parents graciously hosted a small reception in London to introduce my now officially recognised partner to a small gathering of aunts and uncles as well as some of our personal friends (see Figure 3). A few months later we were packed and ready to travel to a new country of which we knew very little beyond the fact that it had attained independence from British colonial rule (as Northern Rhodesia) less than a year ago and was now ruled by an indigenous government headed by the internationally renowned liberation activist, President Kenneth Kaunda, an advocate of multi-racial democracy.

5 Responsibilities of Parenthood and Profession

After some brief explorations of responsibility as a wage earner and as a student activist, in 1965, I embarked on an academic career and travelled abroad with my wife to set up home in a new land. The ensuing phase of my life-journey introduced me to a deeper dimension of responsibility: raising the new person born out of our union as parents. Concurrently, I embarked on a new phase of life as a professional researcher and teacher.

Starting Adult Life in Zambia

Arriving in Zambia was a momentous event in my life. I had read about the university I was joining as a pioneering young academic and about the political struggle for the nation's independence from Britain. I was excited at the prospect of entering a new community, with rather grandiose ideas about how we would be building together a new, post-colonial society free of oppressive, racist laws, and dedicated to meeting the aspirations of the indigenous citizenry. But apart from the fact that they were Africans, I had given no serious thought to what the daily lives of those citizens were like, nor to the specifics of their ecological niche.

> On the last leg of our journey from London to Lusaka, I watched through the porthole window as the plane began its descent. Suddenly a burst of colour came into view – tops of flowering trees, lambent in the midday sunlight with a soft, purplish blue. These, my neighbour explained, were Jacaranda trees. Years later I learned that the Jacaranda trees are not indigenous to Zambia, but were imported from South America, along with a number of other spectacular plants such as the Bourgainvillea, Poinsettia, and Flamboyants that adorn the streets of Lusaka. Nevertheless, I have always treasured them as a distinctive feature of the city which became my home over the next 50 years.

As newcomers to Zambia, we had no established peers or elders to consult about how to adjust. The tiny group of staff recruited to set up the new university came from every corner of the world. Among them we formed friendships with a couple who lived on the same estate as us (Jan and Eva Deregowski) and another couple who had come from Oxford (Edward and Ida Mafethe). Both families, like us, were expecting their first child; so much of our talk was about preparing for child birth and child care. Jan was a Ph.D. student of psychology like me and we became close colleagues in the research of the Human Development Research Unit (HDRU). Edward and I shared a keen interest in the ongoing liberation struggle in his home country, South Africa. We also joined the small, multinational, local chess club. Later we got to meet a number of other families that included children of mixed ethnic heritage, and felt well accepted in the elite stratum of Zambian society.

The university housing allocated to us on arrival was on the small campus of the Institute for Social Research, located next to the famous secondary school for boys, Munali, a few kilometres away from the site established for the construction of the new university. The Institute had a history going back to the 1930s and was internationally renowned as a centre of anthropological research under its former title, the Rhodes Livingstone Institute. Other residents housed on the campus fell into three categories. The Director lived in a grand, two-storey house built to the specifications of a former Director, Henry Fosbrooke, in the 1950s. Various academic staff occupied five family bungalows dating from the 1940s and fitted with modern utilities. And a cluster of much smaller houses served as accommodation for about 20 support staff (clerks, drivers, gardeners, and cleaners) and their families. We lived initially in the smallest of the bungalows, then, after our child was born, in a larger one with an extra bedroom. The offices were centrally located on the campus within a short stroll from any of the houses, and were skirted by a sheltered external corridor, where by tradition mid-morning tea was served.

This was an informal forum at which I interacted with several young social anthropologists, including David Boswell, Bruce Kapferer, and Robin Fielder. Occasionally, the chat-groups would be joined by a senior scholar who shared that disciplinary background and whose publications were based on research in Northern Rhodesia. Notable among these were Max Gluckman and Elisabeth Colson, both former Directors of the Institute. Jan Deregowski and I sometimes felt, as experimental psychologists, like intellectual trespassers in that forum, curious about the nature of indigenous cultural practices that were often discussed, but unconvinced of the methodological adequacy of the research for which the Institute had become famous over the years. I must have seemed naively rigid to many of the anthropologists I met in that period. I recall one particular conversation in which I exclaimed that I couldn't see a qualitative difference between the insights offered by social anthropologists and novelists. Professor Ronald Frankenberg retorted that if he were to publish a good novel he would regard it as the greatest accomplishment of his professional career. The current Director, Alastair Heron, was trained as an experimental psychologist. He had recruited three of us young Ph.D. students to set up a new unit (HDRU) equipped with a dedicated laboratory in a pre-fabricated suite on the campus. Our activities there, conducting tests with children, were reciprocally mysterious to our anthropologist colleagues, whose scepticism about our research methods I only came to appreciate many years later.

Becoming a Father

Our son Derek was born on the same day in March 1966 that the University of Zambia admitted its first students, at the hospital across the road from the Ridgeway Campus where an inaugural series of meetings was held to welcome the new students. I commuted all day between the two venues and in the evening, the Dean of Students, Fergus McPherson, as MC of the event, introduced me as I mounted the platform to address a gathering of students, as 'the new father'. My life-journey as a person over succeeding years ran parallel to and interacted with the life-journey of UNZA as an institution: we grew up together, I from a young scholar recently arrived in Zambia, and UNZA from its embryonic character as an independence project of post-colonial Zambia.

The house into which we brought newborn Derek, located in the grounds of the Institute, had two bedrooms and we set about arranging it as a child-centred home. Esther's preparation for parenthood was grounded in having grown up in a large family, where she had learned to participate in the care and nurturance of her young half-siblings, and in formal training and professional experience as a kindergarten teacher in Singapore and

England. My preparation was devoid of practical experience (personal or professional) and only minimally grounded in scientific theory. The course at Oxford which had introduced me to the kindergarten where I conducted my study of young children provided no theoretical introduction. I had only briefly dipped into the topic of child development in some early publications by Piaget and Vygotsky, neither of whom offered any practical advice on how to manage the life of this astonishing little person. I relied on his mother's intuitive, loving care, supplemented by the latest edition of Benjamin Spock's popular *Baby and Child Care*. One challenge we struggled with was how to manage his plaintive crying when he was tired. We often followed what we took to be authoritative professional advice by letting baby Derek 'cry himself to sleep'. We both found it agonising to refrain from picking him up out of his crib, which was immediately effective in pacifying him. But we told one another that we should hold back in the interest of the child's healthy socioemotional development.

On the cognitive side, I took the opportunity to read carefully Flavell's (1963) recently published compendium of Piaget's research, and was impressed by the precision with which Piaget's detailed 'clinical' observations of his young children matched Derek's behaviour. I also replicated the perceptual preference methods of Fantz (1961), and then seamlessly transitioned into making mobiles to hang over Derek's crib, and an activity board for him to reach out and explore. The vogue of Chomsky's (1965) revolutionary conception of an innate Language Acquisition Device was just beginning at that time, and I paid special attention to Derek's emerging vocabulary and syntax, with daily entries in his baby book. When Esther resumed her career as a teacher at a local school, we engaged a young caregiver to stay with our infant son at home, which was close to my office so that I was able to monitor his care with frequent visits throughout the day. As he grew older, my structured attempts to foster his cognitive development included representational and problem-solving activities: drawing, painting, lego brick construction, and interaction with illustrated storybooks, as well as pre-pilot exploration of various test materials designed for my research. In his adult years, Derek humorously recalled these and later childhood interactions with me as serving as a 'guinea-pig' for his father's experiments! As I put it, more charitably, in the preface to my 1993 book, he and the other four children I co-parented through their early years 'taught me more about developmental psychology than my professional work' (p. xiv). More significant, I now realise, was the opportunity parenting afforded me to learn about taking responsibility. Playing with my own child called for a new kind of responsiveness to the other person's interests and preferences, gauging not only how much he liked a particular stimulus but also where the interaction was leading us, and learning to balance adjusting my behaviour to his demands against leading him towards a goal in his zone of proximal development (Cole, 1985). Responsive play became a favourite mode of interaction with each of my children in the years that followed.

Single Parenthood

The honeymoon period of our marriage was filled with the shared delights and anxieties of raising our baby boy, giving rise to a profound emotional bond between us. But, sadly, after a few years of raising him together, the mutual trust that informed that bond was fractured by emotional challenges that placed intolerable pressure on our interpersonal relationship. In some ways these were reminiscent of the crisis that had driven us apart in England in 1964, but now in 1968 we had much more experience of living together and Esther was more confident in her appraisal of our relationship as unsatisfactory. A tumultuous period of several months ensued, during which we challenged one another with unprincipled candidness to demonstrate our respective desires, causing distress not only to each other but also to many friends and acquaintances. At one point, in desperation, I took an overdose of tranquilisers and ended up in hospital. Eventually, despite my protestations and attempts to negotiate strategies of repair, Esther declared that she could no longer live with me and departed abruptly to England with Derek. I followed her in a state of shock and initiated moves to claim legal parental rights to custody, care, and control of our then three-year-old child. After a few weeks of consulting with lawyers, we agreed to dispense with them and settled on an arrangement under which Derek would return with me to our home in Zambia and would spend a few weeks every year with his mother in England. This agreement was formally recognised by the courts at the time of our divorce in 1971.

Thus, by March 1970, I was living alone with four-year-old Derek close to the university campus. I was one of just two young lecturers staffing the Psychology Department, of similar age to most of my undergraduate students, but accorded a much different level of academic responsibility by virtue of my recently completed Ph.D. degree. I was determined to overcome in one way or another what seemed a failed beginning of adult life. As a father, I knew that I needed to arrange for young Derek to play with other children and explore the physical world. And as a healthy, open-minded young adult, I felt the urge to enjoy interacting with agemates and sharing the excitement of new experiences. My status as a single father was accepted in the student community as somewhat anomalous but generally benign, and I was graciously included in their social life; attending parties; drinking the local lager from the bottle; and dancing to the currently popular mix of Soul music, R&B, and Afrobeat. At one such party I met a young woman who made a powerful impression on me. Hilda was just five years younger than me, but the gap appeared much wider to many of us at the time. I was captivated by her charm, and impulsively embarked on a vigorous courtship, chatting with her in corridors on campus, accompanying her to parties, and introducing her to four-year-old Derek, with whom she quickly formed an affectionate bond (See Figure 4).

Hilda, whose other name Namposya I preferred, was the next to last-born in a family of eight children originating from the 1920s marriage between her parents, who now lived in retirement in a village near Mbala. Her mother was of Mambwe heritage, her father Namwanga. Neither of them had completed more than a few years of formal schooling, but her father had travelled quite widely in the region in his youth, was conversant with English and had become an elder of the African Methodist Episcopal (AME) church. Namposya had moved from her parents' village home, where she completed lower primary school to the small rural town of Luwingu, where she lived with her eldest sister, Lily and brother-in-law, who was the District Secretary, and, after completing upper primary schooling, moved on to secondary school as a boarder in Kasama for five years before qualifying for admission to UNZA in 1969. Both of her elder sisters had married before the Second World War and each had borne a football team of children, many of whom were in Namposya's peer group and currently enrolled in various tertiary educational programmes in Lusaka. She had close, warm relationships with a string of nieces, daughters of her two elder sisters, and I was introduced to all of them.

Some of Namposya's friends and young relatives were quite sceptical about the prospects of our relationship, some emphasising our different cultural origins, others my track history of a broken marriage. As she and I grew closer and began to discuss our feelings for each other, I acknowledged that I had been in love before and had misjudged the resilience of my relationship with Derek's mother. I felt that I had seen much more of the world than her and should not mislead her as to the promise of our love. She, however, gradually convinced me that I was still young enough to make a fresh start. This gesture by Namposya was not directly focused on forgiving the errors of my previous marital relationship. It was a generous vote of confidence in my character's capacity to act more productively in a new relationship with her, and it inspired me to believe more in myself and to embark on a new course of marital partnership, that proved over the years ahead to flourish in ways I had not yet discovered. However, concerned about her vulnerability, I insisted that before making a firm commitment to solidify our relationship into more than a passing affair, I must first formalise my separation from Derek's mother as a permanent

Figure 4 Robert and Namposya jiving in Lusaka – 1970–1972.

divorce. This would require me to spend some time in England working out with Esther a mutually respectful settlement to be presented to the courts, under which we could pursue our separate lives while providing adequate parenting for our child.

I therefore set about looking for a job in England compatible with my professional credentials and my emerging research interests. The institution that responded most positively to my application was the newly established Hester Adrian Research Centre (HARC) at the University of Manchester, where I was appointed to a two-year Research Fellowship to investigate learning processes in children and adults with 'mental handicap' (a designation later renamed *severe learning difficulties*). Consistent with the mandate of the Centre, my research was to be focused on applications of theory to practical issues in the design of education and social services for individuals with severe learning difficulties and their families. The proposal I submitted was informed by the same cognitive theory that had guided my initial research in Zambia, but applied to a population with whom I had no prior experience, and based in a region of England that I had never visited before, the Northwest. My emotions when I set out with Derek to travel by air to Manchester were a mixture of distress at parting with Namposya, apprehension at the prospect of working in a new community where I was unsure of being welcome, and excitement at the prospect of testing whether the theoretical ideas I had been working with could be applied productively to a tangible societal problem.

Applied Research and Parenting in Manchester (1971–1972)

The Director of HARC, Peter Mittler, was a very humane person with first-hand experience of raising a child with a developmental disability and a generous commitment to nurturing a sense of community among the centre staff, who numbered about fifteen. He introduced me to a kind local family to stay with while finding rented accommodation and a kindergarten where Derek could be cared for during my working hours. Derek had become used to both nursery school and home-based care by a nanny in Lusaka, but the facility available in Manchester was completely unfamiliar and he had come to rely on having my company around-the-clock during our transition to Manchester. When I explained that he would need to stay at this new nursery while I went off to work, he became very distraught, and I was equally afflicted by pangs of separation anxiety. However, the staff of the nursery school assured me that his weepy tantrums stopped minutes after my departure, and we soon adjusted to a routine under which we still spent a large part of every day together in a rented house (see Figure 5). In addition to playing ball in the garden and watching TV, our shared activities focused on home-based nurturance of his early literacy learning, mediated by joint storybook reading and a word-building kit that his mother had acquired in her professional work. One day he made a breakthrough, reading aloud to me without any prompting the whole of his favourite Dr Seuss book, *I Do Not Like Green Eggs and Ham*.

My research also focused on literacy instruction, but for a sample of eight–ten-year-olds with minimal language skills attending day classes at a Junior Training Centre (JTC) for children deemed unable to benefit from inclusion in a regular school. I was allocated a space in the Centre which I converted from a linen store into an individual tuition lab. I mapped the task of learning to recognise letters of the alphabet onto two simulated features of the children's regular effective environment: opening a door, and spooning sugar into a cup of tea. The study confirmed some of my theoretical hypotheses, and demonstrated that the children were capable of learning part of the skill of reading if instruction was suitably adjusted to build on their existing competencies. Concurrently, I participated in a collective initiative by the Centre: an evening workshop programme for parents of children with mental handicap. After attending

Figure 5 Robert with young Derek in Manchester 1971

a lecture presentation, participants were divided into small discussion groups where they explored the applicability of the intervention methods presented. A recurrent format in my group was to brainstorm an individualised programme plan (IPP) for a given child whose parents described the child's behaviour and special needs, and who later shared with the group how the IPP had been implemented and with what success. In designing these plans, we drew on the approach to home-based learning programmes of the Portage Project (Bluma et al., 1972), that was currently under development in Wisconsin, USA, for delivering special education to children in sparsely populated rural areas. Consistent with a later review of experience with the Portage method in Britain (Sandow, 1984), I found that some parents in my group were enthusiastic about the structure, while others found it uncomfortable to be cast in the role of a teacher of their child.

Given the limited opportunities afforded by the workshop format for detailed understanding of the children and their individual differences, I decided to follow up with some visits by appointment to the children's homes. One particular case highlighted for me the danger of relying too heavily on parental reports in arriving at a diagnosis and appropriate programme plan.

The parents, an overweight, middle-aged couple with unmistakable affection for their three-year-old son with Down syndrome, reported that he was difficult to feed as he tended to play with the spoon instead of using it to put porridge into his mouth. So we designed an IPP for them to try out during meals. The attending adult would initially hold the child's hand gripping the spoon and guide it to scoop porridge into the child's mouth. Then the support would be gradually faded out, in accordance with the principle of backward chaining. The parents reported that they had followed this programme faithfully over several weeks but with no significant improvement. When I visited the home one mid-morning, I was met by the toddler who had a feeding bottle half full of milk firmly gripped in his mouth. This, I was told, was his regular habit all day between meals! Evidently, we had failed to inquire in our group tutorials whether the child was hungry at the beginning of each meal.

Several thematic principles of my research and practice with children and families during my time at HARC seemed quite innovative in 1971–1972 and later became part of the mainstream of service design for early childhood education and education for children with special needs (CSN). In order to achieve ecological validity, I imported into the everyday school setting familiar features of children's everyday lives: making tea, opening doors. The parent workshops were premised on the significance of parental hands-on experience and expertise as critical features of the environment impacting early childhood development, and as reflections of parental rights.

My sojourn in Manchester occasioned a number of important changes in my outlook on life. I discovered that life as a bachelor was not to my liking. After a few months, I concretised a plan for Namposya to visit me in England. Apart from some tourism of the London 'sights', this afforded important opportunities for me to introduce her to a few of my closest friends, who all signified their approval, and to my mother, who was by then living in retirement in Norfolk. Understandably, given what she had witnessed of my past love affair and marriage, Estelle was cautious, preferring not to explain our relationship to her ageing mother, my Granny. Nevertheless, the visit strengthened my prioritisation of my relationship with Namposya over casual relationships with other women. Consolidation of my parental responsibilities as full-time custodian of Derek gave rise to a growth in personal confidence, and more thoughtful commitment to honouring my social obligations. On the research front, those various changes in my personal outlook laid the ground for a new approach to communication with other parents, moderating the authority derived from technical knowledge with personal humility, respect, and attention to the other party's felt needs.

6 Listening Respectfully, Connecting Locally (Zambia 1972–1989)

In this section, I describe how, in the context of Zambia's early post-colonial aspirations, and of my personal engagement with indigenous cultural norms, I came to realise that my research had been asking a biased set of questions, constrained by the methodological paradigms of my chosen discipline and more broadly by the Western cultural hegemony of modernist philosophy. I resolved, as an aspiring citizen of Zambia, to adopt a different approach, listening more attentively to the voices of indigenous parents and their explanations of how they raise their children. Concurrently, in my personal life, I gradually gained acceptance into Namposya's extended family of origin, as we embarked on nurturing our own nuclear Zambian family.

Arriving in Zambia in the middle of 1972 was a very different experience from my first arrival in 1965. I was pressing a restart button on my career at the University, this time as one of two Lecturers teaching in the embryonic Psychology Department. I was allocated an office on the main campus and a house in a nearby housing estate, Olympia Park. Derek, who had achieved initial English literacy, numeracy, and adjustment to formal classwork during our sojourn in Manchester, was enrolled in the second grade at the nearby public primary school, Northmead. My dominant preoccupation was to restart my love affair with Namposya on a more secure footing. By October, as the Jacaranda trees began to bloom, I was confident enough to propose that we get married. We agreed to hold our wedding in March, following the date set for her graduation from UNZA. The intervening months included intense negotiations to win the approval of her family of origin.

Negotiating Participation

Following indigenous tradition, I enlisted the support of a personal friend, Bernard Kalolo, to act as my *Shimukombe*, a go-between to bring symbolic gifts of a hoe and a plate of maize flour to the parental home. Since her parents lived 1,000 km away in Mbala District, we approached Namposya's big sister in Lusaka. But Eva had already formed a negative opinion of me – a *muzungu* whose habit of wearing tropical sandals in town she considered a sign of dubious respectability, and the formal presentation of traditional gifts did not go well. I tried calling by appointment on her husband in his office, and he solemnly informed me that there was no obstacle under Zambian law to our marriage but that his family were firmly opposed to my proposal. Bernard pointed out that the real authority to accept me into the family lay with Namposya's father and mother in the village, and advised me to approach them directly. So Namposya and I drove up to the village together and she acted as interpreter as I was grilled about the seriousness of my intentions. I explained that I had formally dissolved my previous marriage, had applied for Zambian citizenship, and was committed to building a lasting marriage with Namposya.

Our wedding was distributed over several days and included three strands: a Christian service in the Anglican cathedral, a civil reception modelled after English tradition, and a series of Mambwe-Namwanga rituals conducted at various private residences. The Cathedral was Namposya's regular place of worship and the Dean agreed, after interviewing me about my somewhat unitarian beliefs, to hold the service there, reserving a spot for Namposya's father to add his blessing as an elder of the AME church. For me, the venue was especially pleasing with its beautiful modern architecture. Namposya's brides-maids included two childhood friends, two campus room-mates and an agemate niece, while my best man was my neighbour, UNZA colleague and friend, Sitali Silangwa. Derek was a pageboy and a six-year-old niece, Alice, was a flower-girl. Participation by Namposya's mother in the traditional part of our wedding was especially important for the extended family. It was enacted in conjunction with several elderly aunties through a series of rituals. An overarching theme was 'Remember this: even when you are poor, as husband and wife you should always share what little you have'. Decades later Namposya described her profound experience of the ceremony in an unpublished, autobiographical novel. She also preserved two of the rituals in an elaborated format that she and I enacted on request over the years as a counselling session for several Zambian newly-wed couples.

We understood our commitment to sharing as a married couple to apply not only to material possessions, but also to social responsibilities. Namposya now became Mummy to six-year-old Derek, and we became Mummy and Papa to five-year-old Mwila, whose parents entrusted her to us as a fostered member of our nuclear family, to grow up alongside Derek. A year later, Derek and Mwila welcomed into the family home the first of three additional children conceived from our union: Zewelanji (almost always known as Zewe). Two more children later joined the family: Chisha in 1976 and Namwali in 1980. And when our respective parents grew old, we considered our contribution to their care a joint responsibility.

The ambivalence of the big family into which I married in 1973 changed over time. Some of those who were opposed to including me on grounds of race later became more tolerant as other non-indigenous spouses joined the clan and generated children of 'mixed descent'. Others developed a less xenophobic interest in British culture as they, or their siblings or children travelled abroad for further studies and experienced the challenges of gaining acceptance as immigrants. Out of those progressive changes in the family's collective

Figure 6 Extended family gathering at Institute Director's
Residence, Lusaka 1983.

perspective grew a role for me as uncle or grandpa, and I was treated with commensurate respect at family engagement parties, weddings and funerals. Within the family, I forged deep and enduring friendships with several individuals, including Namposya's younger sister Diana Nampanya, and her cousin and childhood playmate Chisha Mwambazi. Both were both known to me as *mulamu,* a reciprocal term with much stronger connotations of intimacy than the English translation equivalents sister-in-law/brother-in-law. Diana, who qualified as a nurse, lived with us from time to time, and often cared for our children (see Figures 6 and 7). In 1996, when she died prematurely at age 41, we adopted her daughter Suwi as one of ours and brought her to live with us in Baltimore. At the time of our wedding, Chisha was training as a medical doctor in Moscow. Over the years, he and I discovered a shared interest in public health and in 1982 we collaborated when he was Deputy Director at the Zambian Ministry of Health. His daughter Shuko came to live with us for a while and to know me as Papa.

Zambian Languages

One obvious way of listening to the voices of another sociocultural group is to learn their language. Soon after arrival in Lusaka in 1965, I had enrolled in an introductory language course for expatriates offered in the evenings by an indigenous expert in *ciNyanja* (also known as *ciCewa*). Mr. Jere was a methodical teacher,

Figure 7 Family outing in Lusaka mid 1980s: Zewe, Chisha, Namposya and Carla Namwali.

whose classes explained the basic grammar of the language with conjugation exercises similar to those assigned by my Latin teachers at Westminster. The grammatical contrasts between ciNyanja and English were more substantial than those between French and English. I learned that the Bantu languages differed from European languages with respect to inflections and word order, and that the phonology and orthography of ciNyanja were very different from those of my first language (L1) English. This contrastive analysis helped me to understand some of the challenges I faced as a second-language (L2) learner, and I extrapolated the hypothesis that children growing up with ciNyanja as their L1 would be liable to make spelling errors in their L2, English, predictable from the contrast. This hypothesis was confirmed in a study I conducted at several rural primary schools where ciNyanja was the medium of instruction (Serpell, 1968).

My study of 'L1 interference' errors was addressed to explaining the deficient performance of Zambian children on an exogenous task, learning to spell English. The selective attention theory of learning that guided my analysis was narrowly focused on discrimination between similar sounds, without any consideration of the sociocultural parameters of communication within which the languages were deployed in the participants' everyday lives. My study treated language as a purely cognitive domain. But, when I returned to Lusaka in 1972 and began to interact more personally with a wider range of Zambians of various ages, I became more aware of the social and emotional ramifications of language in action. Prompted by interaction with local scholars and a new range of literature, I realised that the sociolinguistic concepts of *code-switching* and *diglossia* were essential for understanding communication and development in a multilingual society. A major source of inspiration for that insight were the occasional seminars of the multidisciplinary Zambia Language Group, established by Mubanga Kashoki on the fringe of the Ford Foundation's ongoing Zambia Language Survey (1970–1971). My paper 'Learning to say it better' (Serpell, 1978), first presented to a Zambian Language Group Conference in Lusaka, reflected a corresponding shift of theoretical focus from my earlier publications. As the group began to engage in 1974–1976 with proposals for national educational reform, I conducted a small systematic study to demonstrate that children entering first grade in Lusaka from Bemba- or Nyanja-speaking families had a multilingual repertoire (Serpell, 1980).

Acknowledging Different Ways of Knowing

In the same year that my doctoral degree was awarded, I came across a short pithy paper by Mallory Wober (1969) entitled 'Distinguishing centri-cultural from cross-cultural tests and research'. In it he argued that most researchers on cognitive development in Africa had unwittingly expressed an ethnocentric attitude by focusing on comparisons with children in the author's home society, posing questions in the form 'how well can they (Africans) do our (European) tricks?'. Instead, a more appropriate research question would be 'how well can they do their tricks?' By likening psychological tests to culture-specific tricks, the paper triggered a realisation that my doctoral research had all fallen into that trap. It also threw a new light on some critical comments by Zambian partici-pants that I had hitherto ignored. For instance, Mrs Ngulube, our research assistant in a study by Gerda Siann (1972) under my supervision, had reported that some of the children exposed to Witkin's Rod-and-Frame test had approached her to complain that the *muzungu* lady was trying to confuse them ('*afuna kutisokoneza*'). And, in one of my psychology courses at UNZA I had exposed students to the binary choice 'game' of my discrimination learning paradigm. In the class discussion that followed, one student noted that the game had a close parallel in his childhood niche, with the notable difference that the leader of the Zambian game deliberately makes the location of the hidden token as unpredictable as possible. I resolved to pay closer attention to the cultural practices of the host community in which I was seeking to find acceptance, observing their spontaneous behaviour and listening to their own interpretations and aspirations.

My first step in that direction was to design a study in which the task of copying an abstract geometrical design by drawing with a pencil on paper was characterised as a culture-specific 'trick' widely mastered by children growing up in a modern Western context but not in the developmental setting of Zambia, and to contrast it with a cognitively similar 'trick' widely mastered in a Zambian developmental setting but unknown in a Western sociocultural context. During my first few years living in Lusaka, I had been impressed by the skills displayed by young boys in the popular play activity of building model cars from strips of wire. But I had not invoked in a systematic study the conceptual similarity of their skills with those of drawing with pencil and paper. In this new experiment, the ostensibly playful activity of building model cars was treated as a context for the display and evaluation of skill analogous to, but different from, the activity of *pattern reproduction* in tests deployed by Western, Gestalt psychologists to study form perception and cognition and incorporated in standardised Western intelligence tests (e.g., Wechsler, 1975), as well as the clinical Bender-Gestalt Test (Shapiro, 1960).

Our experiment was designed to compare the skilled performance by children from different cultural backgrounds on pattern reproduction tasks in those two contrasting representational media: wire-modelling and drawing with a pencil on paper. The items were chosen to be as similar as possible across those and one other medium: clay modelling, a widespread play activity among children in both rural and urban areas across most of sub-Saharan Africa that is very similar in perceptual-motor demands to the activity of modelling in plasticine widespread in homes and schools across the Western world. Two of the items were closely related to items that feature in Western-standardised psychological tests: a square with diagonals and a human figure. Because I had observed Zambian and English children performing such tasks in their regular ecological settings, I was confident of the outcome of the study. But I formalised it as an experiment to test formal hypotheses so as to draw its implications to the attention of the international research community.

In Lusaka I recruited boys and girls enrolled in Grades 2 and 6 at a public primary school, and carefully packed their wire models for safe transportation to England. After settling down in Manchester, I recruited a comparison sample of boys and girls of similar age to the Zambian second-graders at a public primary school serving a low-income neighbourhood, and replicated the procedures. As predicted, the Grade 2 Zambian sample reproduced the patterns much better in the medium of wire modelling than the English children, while the reverse was the case in the pencil and paper medium. Both samples scored equally on reproducing the same patterns in the medium of clay modelling. I submitted a detailed account of this cross-cultural study to the *British Journal of Psychology*, since earlier studies published there had interpreted weak scores by African participants on Western pattern reproduction tasks as evidence of some kind of broad perceptual or cognitive deficit. My report, which proposed an alternative explanation in terms of context-specific skills, was accepted for publication and has been widely cited in the scientific literature (Serpell, 1979).

The Katete Project

A second response to Wober's charge of ethnocentrism in Western research on child development in Africa is more radical. Rather than focusing on measuring performance with more ecologically relevant tasks, perhaps we should begin by establishing what are the goals of child development most highly valued in African communities and families. In order to capitalise on my sketchy famil-iarity with *ciNyanja*, I sought an introduction to a rural *CiCewa*-speaking community in Katete District, 300 km from Lusaka. An UNZA student who had grown up in the area introduced me to a local primary school teacher, Mr Masiye, who accompanied me to several nearby villages. At my request, he explained the purpose of my visit as follows: I was a teacher at the big school in Lusaka, the University of Zambia. But I had not come here to teach. I had come to learn, from them, the people of Katete, how they raise their children. This set the tone for a relationship between me as researcher and informants indigenous to the host community characterised by egalitarian discourse.

I set out to consult indigenous owners of the cultural system of meanings in such a way as to focus their attention on what they do in their daily interactions with children, away from the immediate influence of culturally exogenous practices, and how they decide on alternative courses of action. I wanted to avoid ending up with an analysis that was more about words than about the ideas they are deployed to represent (Serpell, 1977). So I tried to design a set of hypothetical scenarios in which individual differences are key to successful participation, representing emergency situations rather than routine events, yet clearly identifiable as plausible within the local eco-cultural context. I recruited the support of personal friends and colleagues familiar with Zambian village life to brainstorm such scenarios. My wife Namposya also contributed ideas based on her experience of growing up in a subsistence agricultural village in the north before embarking on her successful journey of formal education. One of the scenarios we adopted was as follows:

> Suppose you are down by the river washing clothes with these children, and you see that the place where you usually spread out the clothes to dry has been soiled by wild animals. Which of these children would you send to find a new place suitable for laying out clothes to dry?

Other scenarios referred to responding to an accidental fire, repairing a roof, and carrying a message to a neighbouring village. Once a respondent had designated a particular child, we followed up with open-ended questions about why she or he had selected that child, and recorded the response in terms of the informant's own preferred relevant terminology.

Analysis of the terms used by our informants to explain their selections gave rise to the insight that the Cewa concept of *nzelu* (intelligence) comprises two complementary dimensions: *cenjela* (cleverness, or cognitive alacrity) and *tumikila* (social responsibility). When we asked the same informants which of the two dimensions is more important, they consistently replied that both are important, and a child without either does not qualify for the designation of *nzelu*. Findings of the study were reported piecemeal in a series of conference presentations and journal articles between 1974 and 1989. But a full integration was not published until the field work was completed. The lessons that I learned from the project are discussed further in my book (1993a) *The Significance of Schooling*, which I finished writing during the first part of our family's sojourn in Baltimore. Several studies in other African cultures (e.g., Dasen et al., 1985; Grigorenko et al., 2001) have reached similar conclusions about the importance attached to social responsibility as an integral feature of intelligence.

The Significance of Schooling in Zambian Society

My research project in Katete was initially titled 'Intelligence, education and adaptation in a rural community', and supported with a small internal research grant from UNZA. Having concluded that the criteria by which local Chewa villagers were estimating the intelligence of the children growing up in their community differed from those informing systematically developed psychological tests, I wondered which of these two perspectives would be more predictive of children's success in mastering the formal school curriculum. The best available measure of that success seemed to be the nationally standardised Secondary School Selection Examination (SSSE), administered every year at the end of Grade 7 in all public schools across the country. The children in my sample ranged in age from six to fourteen and in years of schooling completed from 0 to 3. So, in order to compare their SSSE scores, I would need to wait for a number of years until they had all reached the grade in which they would be eligible to sit for the exam. I revisited the neighbourhood once a year in order to stay in touch with the families and keep track of their children.

As the years went by, the focus of my study expanded to a broader analysis of the relations between schooling and the life-journeys of my cohort of twenty-seven boys and nineteen girls. In 1974, the majority of these children had spent a few years in school but had dropped out before reaching Grade 7. Twelve boys, but none of the girls, had sat for the Grade 7 exam, and only two of those candidates had completed the full five-year secondary curriculum. Eight girls and six boys had never enrolled in school at all. Teachers at the local school reported that every year they went door-to-door trying to persuade parents to enrol their children in Grade 1, but with only limited success despite the availability of places. This was quite surprising to some of my contacts at the Ministry of Education in Lusaka, some of whom suggested that my sample was rather atypical. For them, the big picture was that demand for schooling in the post-independence period had been consistently high, as evidenced by the long queues outside schools in the cities every January as parents sought to enrol their children. However, several other studies in rural areas (Colson, 1971; Eisemon, 1989) have confirmed that the national self-appraisal of a people hungry for education is a simplification that needs to be unpacked to acknow-ledge that many parents in rural communities are sceptical of the value of local formal schooling, on the grounds that its practices do not effectively promote some of their indigenous values, such as interpersonal respect and social responsibility.

In addition to documenting the timeline of enrolment in schooling by each individual member of the cohort, our study explored the significance of schooling from various perspectives. For some local participants schooling represented an opportunity for youth to appropriate new, socially transforma-tive ideas. But for others it dwelt too heavily on imparting technical skills with little local relevance, instead of cultivating indigenous values such as *nzelu*: socially responsible intelligence. The life-journeys we tracked varied across individual participants, with schooling influencing their decisions at various junctures in diverse ways that extended beyond the school's definition of success as extraction from the local community into a higher, predominantly urban domain.

Accounting to the Host Community

While it was clear to me that teachers, parents, and pupils often interpreted specific behaviours differently, I was unsure of the most effective way of communicating that insight to different audiences in an enlightening or empowering way. We made two systematic attempts to share findings of our research with the host community. The first was a set of feedback seminars, conducted in *ciCewa* in each of seven villages, by the school headmaster and local representatives of the government health and agricultural services. My UNZA student research assistants, who had both grown up locally, distributed some written examples of our research findings, citing verbatim quotations from village adults about the benefits and shortcomings of local schooling in the local domains of agriculture and health. Despite our elaborate attempts to facilitate an egalitarian exchange of views, the students' records revealed that the discussions were dominated by criticism and exhortation of parents by the school headmaster and health officer. Moreover, women villagers, who had engaged critically with these topics in our audiotaped family conversations, remained essentially passive in these more public discussions.

Disappointed with this outcome, I later adopted a quite different approach, inspired by the work of Dr Penina Mlama, a distinguished practitioner and theorist of popular theatre in Tanzania, that had generated salience for the voices of women in marginalised rural communities similar to the one that had hosted our work in Zambia (cf. Mlama, 1991). Following her advice, I recruited a colleague at UNZA, Dr Mapopa Mtonga (also internationally renowned in the use of popular theatre to promote social development) to join me in assembling a team of actor/animateurs to travel to Katete and explore the potential of their method for achieving a better way of sharing with the community what we had learned from our research. What emerged was a drama, composed on site, that drew creatively on the imagery of an indigenous repertoire of symbols deployed by a local secret society (*gule wamkulu*) traditionally charged with preparing Cewa boys for adulthood (Mtonga, 1980). The drama wove together the lives of a boy and a girl with contrasting views on the value of schooling. In addition to professional actors in the visiting team, the cast included some locally recruited adults and school children. These were assigned roles in the drama that were very different from their real-world occupational status in the host community. The drama was performed in the open, and attracted a large audience of local adults and children. Audience reaction was enthusiastic. Informal evaluation was compiled by the cast who mingled with the audience as they dispersed, and relayed the thrust of overheard conversations that evening to the research team. It was clear that both leading characters in the play had elicited empathy, and that women were as outspoken as men in their comments on the morals of the story.

Comparing the drama with the seminars, it struck me that the two forms had different requirements as media for communication (Serpell, 1993a, p. 243). Our objective for the seminars was to generate analytical consensus, leading in due course to policy change, and policy implementation. But for the drama, our objectives were to elicit empathy, to raise consciousness, and to promote adoption of responsibility. The two ways of sharing with the host community the findings of the research represented different, complementary ways of communicating knowledge and opinion, reflecting different understandings of the relations between research and sociocultural change.

7 Intimate Family Culture and Parenting in the USA (Baltimore 1990–2002)

In the 1990s, I was based as a sojourner in the USA, with institutional responsibilities at the public University of Maryland, Baltimore County (UMBC), charged with promoting cultural diversification of a programme of graduate studies in Applied Developmental Psychology (ADP). In collaboration with a new set of colleagues, I set about recruiting students with a minority or international background, developing a curriculum responsive to their diverse experiences and interests, and generating a collaborative, five-year longitudinal study of literacy development. The study focused on a cohort of children entering public preschool classes in the 1990s in contrasting eco-sociocultural niches within the historically troubled city of Baltimore. The research design built on and extended the methods of the Katete study described in Section 6 to investigate parental ethnotheories. The personal life of our nuclear family faced numerous challenges in adapting to American society. Many of these were productive and enriching. But one of them came as a terrible shock and threw us into disarray.

Diverse Ways of Becoming Literate in an American City

The Early Childhood Project, co-directed with Drs Linda Baker and Susan Sonnenschein, was given its name to emphasise that our focus on literacy development was situated within the lives of whole children and their families, not just the demands of the school curriculum. A major goal of our study was to probe beneath social address labels, and explore the intimate culture of each child's family home. Within our sampling frame of children attending public preschools and primary schools in the racially fragmented city of Baltimore, we selected equal numbers representing each of four social addresses: low-income African-American, low-income European-American, middle-income African-American, middle-income European-American. In addition to multiple assessments of each child's competencies over three-to-five years, their home was visited repeatedly to document in detail its recurrent activities with qualitative and quantitative analysis of parental reports: caregiver ethnotheories (Serpell et al., 1991; Serpell et al., 1997); ecological inventories (Sonnenschein, Baker & Serpell, 1995); and coded analysis of videotaped parent–child interactions at home (Baker et al., 2001). Most of the fieldwork was implemented by a team of graduate students of various ethnocultural origins who concurrently grounded their individual theses and dissertations (seventeen in all) in data collected for the project. Regular meetings of the whole team afforded enriching opportunities for brainstorming approaches and methods of entry into children's homes and engagement with their parents, as well as hands-on methods of eliciting evidence of the children's emergent literacy in the contexts of their homes and schools.

Building on and refining the methods developed in the Katete project for investigating parental ethnotheories, we structured our data collection around a sequence of inquiries beginning with a 'diary' to be kept by each child's primary caregiver (usually the mother) in the form of entries in a notebook or on a cassette tape-recorder. Each caregiver maintained a daily record of the child's activities for a week, from which we selected particular topics for further elaboration in a series of face-to-face interviews. We sought to promote an egalitarian discourse by opening each discussion of child-rearing practices and values with an open-ended invitation to the individual informant to specify in her own words what the various recurrent activities she had reported meant to the child and to the adult. Using this bottom-up approach led us to the conclusion that across the four social addresses, intellectual goals commanded lower priority than social, moral, and personal goals when the child was in preschool, but that the emphasis shifted in favour of intellectual goals by the time the child was enrolled in the third grade of primary school. We also conducted an ecological inventory of each home, documenting through observations and interviews details of the child's everyday experience, in terms of activities we considered supportive of the child's literacy development (games and play activities, meal-time activities, TV and radio activities, recurrent outings, and reading, writing, and drawing activities).

Analysis of the ecological inventories, diaries and parental ethnotheory interviews revealed two broadly contrasting perspectives on the best way for a family to support their child's early acquisition of literacy. One conceived literacy as a set of skills that should be deliberately cultivated, while the other conceived literacy as a source of entertainment. According to the entertainment perspective, the key to early literacy development is motivation. Children's interest in stories and other written information motivates them to master the written code and adults can leverage that interest by providing plenty of child-friendly samples of print. Moreover, the central purpose of reading is to retrieve meaning from print, and that is made clearer in activities that focus on the pleasures of reading than by heavy emphasis on mastery of the writing code. This entertainment perspective was more often expressed by the middle-class and European-American parents in our sample and, independent of their family's social address, it was correlated with stronger literacy performance by the children on a wide range of indicators (Sonnenschein et al., 1997). Reflecting on the only partial correlation of this pair of contrasting orientations with either social class or ethnicity, we settled on the construct of a family's intimate culture with its own unique constellation of characteristics.

Our interviews with teachers in the various classes in which our sample of children were enrolled over the years were conducted by the principal investigators of the project and were relatively unstructured. A thematic analysis of the audiotape records by Dr Jalil Akkari, an anthropologist attached to the project team for a year, revealed some systematic differences between the two ethnocultural groups of teachers interviewed: African-American teachers displayed a stronger attachment to the theme of 'universal educability', while European-American teachers placed more emphasis on the theme of 'responsibility of a teacher' (Akkari et al., 1998).

Interpreting group differences in perception and understanding of a child's development became a preoccupation for me as I was completing my book about the Katete project and informed much of the brainstorming with my American colleagues as we designed the Baltimore Early Childhood Project. A wide-ranging philosophical and metatheoretical paper that I prepared in the late 1980s, in response to an invitation from the editor, elicited such divided reactions among expert peer reviewers that he declined to publish it. With the support of several colleagues, I prepared an extensive revision, and it was eventually published in a rather obscure newsletter (Serpell, 1990). The core theoretical idea, which I have restated and further elaborated in a number of subsequent publications (Serpell, 1994, 2006, 2020), is that psychological interpretation is a reflexive process that presupposes logically that the three participants in a communication could exchange positions of author, audience, and human subject (see Figure 8)

The three positions on the diagram arise from the logic of communication: an author addresses a speech utterance to an audience about a subject. The author identifies an ostensible subject as referent and proposes to the audience an

Figure 8 The reflexive triangle (Serpell 1990).

interpretation of the behaviour and mind of that subject, who also has a perspective of her own. The perspectives symbolised by overlapping circles in the figure should be interpreted not as socioemotionally neutral, static descriptions of the objective world but as representations of that world that are advanced as bids for representational interaction in which considerations of power and honesty are also at play (Serpell, 2020, p. 2).

Adolescence and Emerging Adulthood of Our Children in America

The intimate culture of our nuclear family that migrated with me to Baltimore in 1989 had evolved from its 1973 foundation in Lusaka to incorporate the experiences of two sojourns abroad (New York and Hawaii, 1976–1977; and Hull, 1983–1984). Derek (aged 23) and Mwila (22) had embarked on their adult life-journeys elsewhere, leaving just the three sisters, Zewe, Chisha, and Carla, to co-construct with Namposya and me a family niche for ourselves as newcomers to Maryland, USA.

Zewe was fifteen and completed her last two years of formal education at a well-reputed public school in our suburb of Baltimore (Pikesville High) before proceeding in 1992 to university studies at Clark University in Massachusetts, where she graduated *summa cum laude* in 1996. Carla was 9 and started in Grade 3 at a neighbourhood public elementary school, moved on to the local middle school and then to a selective magnet programme for gifted and talented students embedded within a troubled public high school in the city. From there she proceeded on a competitive scholarship to university studies at Yale in 1998, where she decided to go by her middle name, Namwali. Both Zewe and Namwali went on later to complete PhD degrees at American universities and to build successful careers in academia. Chisha was thirteen and enrolled at the same school as Zewe, one year behind. She was a vivacious and temperamental spirit with a keen interest in visual art. Her experience at Pikesville High gave rise to a traumatic series of episodes that extended into her life at several colleges. When Suwi, following the untimely death of her mother in Zambia in 1997, joined us in Baltimore, she was eight years old and had just started learning to read. The administrative challenges of adoption and migration led to her being enrolled in a series of different schools, but she integrated rapidly, mastering spoken English and soon forgot her first language Bemba, which was seldom spoken in our home. However, because she was a decade or more younger that the other three girls, her status in the family came to resemble that of a grandchild.

We, the parents, also experienced formative personal experiences outside the home, that impacted in significant ways on the family's collective life. My

Figure 9 Family outing in Baltimore: Afram Festival 1992 – Namposya, Zewe, Carla Namwali & Chisha.

professional activities and development are described elsewhere in this Element. Namposya was registered as a Ph.D. student in the Policy Sciences programme at UMBC, graduating in 1999. Building on her doctoral research, she developed an international career in policy and management of services for children in Africa affected by the AIDS pandemic, initially based in Washington, DC, and traveling extensively. Her familiarity with evidence-based agenda-setting and policy implementation earned her respect both in the global professional culture of the international NGOs and in local settings as a working mother. Accompanying the children as they engaged with African dances and European paintings at the Baltimore Museum of Art and various centres in Washington, DC, gave me a sense of constructive continuity in the evolving cosmopolitan culture of our family, that resonated with the academic debates of my professional life. We seemed to be well placed to celebrate America's mixed cultural heritage (see Figure 9). Moving from Zambia to the USA required major adaptations on the part of each of us, including the children's access to education. The texture of our family's everyday life wove together, unselfconsciously, strands of various cultural practices that we had picked up in Zambia, England, or the USA. Our everyday conversations ranged widely over multiple cultural traditions, citing historical events and issues commonplace in any one of the societies as relevant examples to throw light on an immediate topic of current local interest, and invoking proverbial explanations prevalent in any one of those societies. Often a linguistic expression in French or in one of the Zambian languages would be thrown into the flow of a predominantly English sentence, in the manner characterised in sociolinguistic theory as 'translanguaging'.

The Pleasure Traps of Alcohol and Drugs

In the wild years of my early adulthood, I had regarded alcohol consumption as a pleasurable practice, whose suppression in Islamic states and during the Prohibition period of US history were ideologically extremist infringements on personal liberty. When my teaching responsibilities at UNZA led me in the 1980s to read the scientific literature, it came as a rather shocking revelation to discover that alcohol is classified in medicine as a poison. As a cognitive psychologist, it struck me that I had ignored the objectively depressant action of alcohol on the central nervous system and consequential impairment of judgment. I realised I had been duped by social convention and commercial advertising into regarding alcohol as a benign substance and interpreting conspicuously negative behaviours following its consumption as primarily due to excess. Looking back, I recognised that my behaviour around alcohol had often been irresponsible, including driving under its influence, and resolved to adhere strictly to the mantra 'don't drink and drive'. Sadly, I witnessed a number of Zambian friends struggle with the challenge of moderating their alcohol intake. Some eventually decided to opt for total abstinence, while others narrowly escaped disastrous consequences in the context of driving or of marital conflict. I myself enjoyed alcohol socially and only occasionally regretted having drunk too much. I also experimented briefly with *mbanji* (the local word for cannabis) but experienced a disconcertingly extreme loss of cognitive self-control and resolved to stay away from it.

However, hard drugs and addiction lay beyond my personal experience until I moved to Baltimore, where I came face-to-face with the evil of exploitative marketing and its tragic impact on vulnerable adolescents. Public discourse about the topic was much less salient in Zambia than in the USA. I recall that I dismissed as alarmist the warning by an American friend in Zambia who, on learning that I had secured the appointment at UMBC, said with a sadly ironic smile 'you do realise, I suppose, that you are moving with your family to the heroin capital of the world?' After arrival, Namposya and I were alarmed by repeated warnings in the media, and we decided to sit our two older girls down for a serious talk soon after they had started at Pikesville High School. We flagged two issues as the agenda for this family *indaba*. What were they hearing and observing at school about (a) academic cheating and (b) drug abuse? The girls both acknowledged that they had come across the phenomena at school, and found them alien to their Zambian cultural orientation. They expressed strong distaste and disapproval for both, especially cheating: 'why would anyone want to earn a grade dishonestly ? what would be the point?!' They assured us that they understood the danger of hard drugs and that they were adamant in their refusal of all the offers they had received from schoolmates to try them. Unwisely complacent, we placed only limited constraints on the girls' social lives, encouraging them to accept invitations to visit the homes of school friends and to join innocent-sounding group outings with other, local teenagers.

One recurrent theme for each of the girls, as fresh arrivals from Zambia, was affirmation of her personal identity: was she African, biracial, Black, African-American? Her chosen answer served as one of several clues to the puzzle of how to fit in at school, alongside and interacting with learning the formal rules of the institution (how to please the teacher) and the informal conventions of how to speak, how to dress, and how to respond to teasing. The demographic profile of the high school was predominantly Jewish, reflecting the composition of the residential zone it was mandated to serve. This contrasted with the profile of other nearby schools. The catchment zones of public schools were strictly defined, coinciding with silent boundaries between higher and lower socioeconomic class neighbourhoods, rationalised on the basis of tax rates levied by local government authorities. Although race was not a criterion in public discourse, the *de facto* segregation of Pikesville, which fell within Baltimore County, from the adjacent, predominantly African-American neighbourhood of Washington Heights inside the city boundary meant that any dark-complexioned child attending Pikesville High was often suspected of being an outsider who was somehow cheating the system.

We only learned in fits and starts from the children how each of them negotiated the challenges and frustrations of life in the fragmented eco-sociocultural system of Baltimore. Zewe firmly defined herself as Black, surrounding herself with African-American friends. Carla, still relatively young, had a more eclectic approach, making friends at school with peers of various ethnic backgrounds. Chisha also seemed at first open to forming friendships with Jewish as well as African-American peers, but took to clandestinely exploring social life in the city, and was lured into the pleasure trap of psychotropic drugs – a fact we only discovered several years later. She was still quite young at high school graduation in 1994. So we encouraged her to take a break before proceeding to New York University, where she had qualified for admission. Things came to a head in her first semester there in 1995 when it became apparent that her drug abuse was interfering with her studies. We brought her home to live with us during our year back in Lusaka, and she enrolled successfully in some courses at UNZA in 1996, followed by a spell of part-time studies at UMBC in 1997–1998. But she never managed to overcome her addiction, prompting a series of clinical interventions, including spells of several weeks in residential treatment centres. By 1999, the family had become used to her instability, but we were all unprepared for her sudden demise due to an accidental drug overdose.

Losing Chisha was for each of us parents an irreparable personal loss. For our nuclear family it was a catastrophic amputation: an organic part of our everyday functioning was no longer there. I felt an overwhelming sense of shame at my failure as a parent. Namposya and I realised there was a danger of the tragedy invading our marital relationship, poisoning it with recrimination and mistrust, and resolved not to let that happen. Entrusting the other children to one another's care, we parents travelled together to Zambia, and carried Chisha's ashes with us. She had intimated several years ago that she would rather be cremated than buried, and respecting that wish seemed a self-evident obligation. Rather than deal with the expectations of the extended family regarding funeral arrangements, we resolved to scatter our daughter's ashes in the wilderness at a place of exceptional natural beauty close to the family's original village homestead in Mbala District. Namposya's two eldest sisters were now resident nearby, and they agreed to accompany us to the Kalambo Falls, where we took turns to scatter Chisha's ashes over the precipice into the wind. The long journey by air and road afforded us long hours in which to share our emotions, and we resolved to find a way to move forward as a couple, sharing responsibility for continuing care of the children who had survived. Looking back two decades later, against the backdrop of her siblings' successful transitions into adulthood, the tragedy of Chisha's life-journey ending at the age of twenty-two still haunts me as a promise unfulfilled.

Transition Back to Zambia

It was not immediately apparent to Namposya and me that we would move back to Zambia, and we explored a number of other avenues. We no longer felt at ease in Baltimore and I interviewed unsuccessfully for several academic positions at other universities in the USA and abroad. After about three years had passed, a unique opportunity arose to embark on a career move I had never considered. The position of Vice-Chancellor of the University of Zambia was advertised, and two trusted Zambian academic friends urged me to apply. I had already made arrangements to spend a year of sabbatical leave at the nearby University of Malawi, and along the way we hosted the wedding of our eldest daughter Zewe in Lusaka. So, when the search committee shortlisted me as a candidate, I was able to drive from Zomba to Lusaka for interview. I called on a number of respected former UNZA colleagues to sound them out privately about my suitability for the job and received encouragement. The search committee arranged for me to make my case to a select audience of staff and students and soon after my return to Malawi they phoned to offer me appointment. I was apprehensive but also excited, and had the support of Namposya, who was just getting started in a professionally fulfilling job with an American NGO that deployed her frequently to Malawi. I requested the Zambian Minister of Education (the appointing authority) to write to UMBC and the University of Malawi to release me from my contractual obligations so as to start work as UNZA's new VC on 1 January 2003.

8 Engagement with Progressive Social Change (Zambia, Baltimore 1980–2006)

In this Section, I describe several different activities that brought me out of the role of scholar as observer into a more practically engaged role, combining technical analysis with moral commitment to promote an agenda of social change. The first was a consulting activity that morphed into an advocacy process. During my term as Director of the Institute for African Studies (1977–1983), I led a technical support team for the government's National Campaign to Reach Disabled Children. My understanding of the interface between scientific theory, professional practices, and public policy was profoundly influenced by my participation in the campaign. A second major opportunity for practical engagement arose in the USA with my appointment as Director of UMBC's graduate studies programme in Applied Developmental Psychology (1989–2002), where I was charged with promoting the diversification of student enrolment. In 1995–1996, I began a mixed-methods case study of a grassroots, teacher-led action project of curriculum innovation at a public primary school in northern Zambia, inspired by the concept of Child-to-Child. I studied the implementation and impact of the project with two UNZA colleagues (Gertrude Mwape and Tamara Chansa-Kabali) and two UMBC graduate students (Adamson-Holley 1999; Udell, 2001) over a period of eight years. My most explicitly managerial experience of engagement was as Vice-Chancellor of UNZA (2003–2006), with responsibility for implementation of programmatic institutional change at the national university. This vantage point raised my awareness of the challenges of communication with multiple stakeholders that became an enduring preoccupation of my approach to international issues.

The Zambia National Campaign to Reach Disabled Children (ZNCRDC 1981–1983)

The United Nations declared 1981 the International Year of Disabled Persons, calling for a plan of action at national, regional, and international levels, focused on equalisation of opportunities, rehabilitation, and prevention of disabilities. The professional terminology of *handicap*, prevalent at the time of my work in Manchester in the seventies, gave way around this time to a view of *disability* as a three-level process (Susser, 1990), beginning with organic *impairment*, that leads unless checked to functional *disability*, which in turn can cause a social *handicap*, unless prevented. Primary interventions such as obstetric care, optimising nutrition, or supplementation of iodine can reduce the incidence of impairments, while prosthetic and assistive technology and special education can reduce secondary disabilities, and social engineering can mitigate tertiary handicaps.

Assessment as a Guide to Action

One of the activities proposed by UNICEF in Zambia was a systematic estimation of the prevalence of various types of childhood disability, as a basis for projecting service needs. Discussion in the national planning committee recognised that for accurate assessment parental reports would need to be complemented by professionally guided *ascertainment*, and that mere head-counting would be unethical given the paucity of existing services. Hence, the initiative was formulated as not just a descriptive survey, but a campaign to reach and try to assist the families of children with severe needs. Ascertainment of such needs would involve deploying adequately skilled personnel to conduct assessment as a guide to action (Serpell & Nabuzoka, 1991). The Institute was commissioned to establish a technical support team to advise on logistics and this grew into a major preoccupation for me through the end of my term as Director and beyond. Three principles guided the team's applied research and development. The assessment procedures should be manageable by personnel with limited professional training; they should generate an individualised action plan on the child's behalf; and recommended interventions should, as far as possible, be feasible for families with limited resources within the local community. A multisectoral team of three Ascertainment Officers was appointed for deployment in each of the nation's fifty-seven Districts, and we designed a two-week crash course to train them in screening procedures and registration of each child ascertained as having one or more types of severe functional disability, culminating in a Provisional Care Plan (Serpell & Jere-Folotiya, 2011).

Policy Priorities: Quality and Access

Expert analysis of the data collected over six months, comprising 7,100 children aged five to fifteen registered as severely disabled, gave rise to an estimated prevalence of about 2.2 per cent. This was much lower than the widely touted UN ballpark estimate of 10 per cent, but also well beyond the current capacity of the nation's special educational provision. At that time, a total of 1,200 children aged five to fifteen were currently enrolled in special schools and units, and even doubling that enrolment would only have catered for 2,400 of the 36,000 severely disabled children estimated by the campaign (Nabuzoka, 1986). These statistics were interpreted as confirming the WHO policy position that continuing the current practice of providing 'institutional' education in specialised centres (IBR) did not have the potential to provide affordable, immediate coverage of the majority of needy children and their families. A much more feasible way forward was Community Based Rehabilitation (CBR, Helander et al., 1980), relying on the family and local neighbourhood for implementation of any professionally recommended service provision. Moreover, I contended, such community-based services at their best had a number of other strategic advantages: acknowledging and fostering family commitment to the child's welfare, cultivating parental confidence in meeting their child's needs, focusing on the child as a whole person, recruitment of community involvement in the rehabilitation process, and ensuring continuity of care over the child's lifetime (Serpell, 1986).

Implementation Constraints

The three Government Ministries that had participated in the campaign needed to reflect on the implications of this radical recommendation and to consult with the various local specialists, many of whom were sceptical of the feasibility of mobilising parents and communities to provide relevant support for children with severe disabilities (Miles, 1985). We realised belatedly that we had side-lined those experts in the design of the campaign, and yet they were crucial stakeholders in any programme of policy reform. A series of consultative meetings was convened, culminating in a national workshop at which the encouraging findings of two six-month pilot studies were presented that deployed an itinerant District CBR team staffed by the former Ascertainment Officers under the guidance of a trained professional. A bridge was proposed between such itinerant teams and the more expert personnel of existing special-ised centres. The meeting was generally impressed with the feasibility of a national CBR strategy, provided adequate funding could be secured, and the Ministry of Health was assigned to take a lead in implementation (Nabuzoka, 1986). Despite this apparent progress towards national consensus-building, the momentum of evidence-based policy reforms declined abruptly between 1985 and 1989, perhaps because of the loss of strategic focus following dissolution of the Technical Support Team at UNZA. Two decades later, reflecting on why the shift in policy towards CBR, proposed to the government in 1983 had not been translated into practice, several obstacles were identified: a lack of financial resources during the economic recession of the 1990s, and upstaging of the needs of children with disabilities by the Girl Child initiative and the World Bank policy emphasis on expanding access to basic education (Serpell & Jere-Folotiya, 2011). In the Salamanca Declaration (UNESCO, 1994), international policy took a step further the critique of institutionalisation and underlined the fundamental importance of inclusion as a basic human right often denied to persons with disabilities. But the momentum generated by the ZNCRDC in the 1980s was not invoked by the Zambian government in its official endorsement of the principle of educational inclusion.

Child-to-Child

The Child-to-Child (CtC) approach of mobilising children to engage actively in health-promotion in their families and communities was publicised in the 1960s under the auspices of the International Year of the Child (Pridmore, 1996). While the prime movers, David Morley and Hugh Hawes, were British-born, they both drew inspiration from their observation, when working in several non-Western societies, that children routinely participated actively in care of their infant siblings. To leverage that cultural practice in the context of Primary Health Care, a programmatic focus sought to embed the CtC concept within the curriculum of basic/primary schooling under the heading of health education (Hawes & Scotchmer, 1993). A coordinating centre was established at the University of London Institute of Education and funding secured under a Trust. From the outset, Hawes and Morley emphasised that resources for the implementation of CtC should be generated from the bottom upwards by practitioners working in Third-World countries (www.childtochild.org.uk/), and they resisted as best they could its drift towards definition as a First-World centre generating plans and principles to be distributed to a subordinate periphery.

Although I was familiar with the 1978 Alma Ata Declaration on Primary Health Care, I had not heard about the Child-to-Child concept until William

Figure 10 Mother teaching her pre-adolescent daughter to carry baby sister on her back (*papu*) – Mpika 1997.

Gibbs, a former Lecturer at a Zambian College of Education, drew my attention to a CtC initiative in Zambia's predominantly rural, Northern Province. A group of primary school teachers were spearheading the initiative, making innovative use of the Under-5 Growth Chart as an instructional resource (Morley & Woodland, 1988). During my year of sabbatical leave from UMBC (1995), I recruited a colleague on the staff of the UNZA Psychology Department, Gertrude Mwape, to help initiate a study of this educational innovation at a government primary school in Mpika.

Our first visit to Kabale School was hosted by Clement Mumbo and Paul Mumba. Their enthusiasm was inspiring. They expressed a strong sense of ownership of the approach, which they believed had revolutionised their teaching. They articulated philosophical principles, explained practical details of the activities they were putting in place to encourage young learners to collaborate, and described positive learning outcomes. They welcomed the opportunity for a research and practice partnership with the university, which generated over the years a number of reports and peer-reviewed publications (Mwape & Serpell, 1996; Mumba, 2000; Serpell, 2008; Serpell, Mumba, & Chansa-Kabali, 2011; Serpell & Adamson-Holley, 2016). Our overall evaluation was that the approach had successfully built on an existing indigenous socialisation practice (See Figure 10) to enrich the primary school curriculum, enabling young learners to make a valuable immediate impact on the local community (see Figure 10), and sowing seeds of social responsibility that gave tangible fruit in their adult lives.

I never really joined the CtC 'club', but I found the label convenient for both the 'movement' and the key concept informing it. However, when I asked other people about it in the late 1990s, both at the local level in Mpika and at the national level in Lusaka, I found that CtC had been 'projectised' in the public imagination, as an activity in Mpika, funded by UNICEF some years back, completed and superseded in significance by other funded projects like The Girl Child. Yet the relevance of the concept that children can be effective and easily motivated agents of healthcare has been recognised as resonating with indigenous child rearing practices in several African societies. Bame Nsamenang, with whom I became friends in 1989, emphasised in his pioneering study of the Nso people of Western Cameroon, that 'the extent of child-to-child socialisation of skills, affect, and cognition is substantial; perhaps far more extensive and developmentally more critical than direct parental <socialization>' (Nsamenang & Lamb, 1993). Over the course of our later collaboration on the refinement of early childhood education interventions in Africa, Nsamenang and I have often articulated the case that this is a social practice with a coherent cultural rationale of priming pre-adolescents for the responsibilities of parenthood later in their lives (Serpell & Nsamenang, 2015). It has been widely misinterpreted by international development agencies as oppressive of girls. But we have argued to the contrary that it is something Europe and North America can learn from other societies in the Majority World.

Diversification of Research and Higher Education in the USA

When I moved from Zambia to the USA in 1989, my long-term aspiration was to establish at UNZA, or at another centre of higher education and research in Africa, a strong enough programme of doctoral studies to attract talented students from African countries in the region. I had circulated a concept paper in preceding years, arguing that relevant applied research on African child development should be led by African scholars trained and based on the continent, and that only a regional centre would be able to attract a critical mass of qualified faculty in the specialised field of child development. It became clear to me that the credibility of my argument would benefit from some first-hand experience of supervising doctoral research. So the Directorship of UMBC's graduate studies programme in Applied Developmental Psychology (ADP) appealed to me as an opportunity to gain such credentials, albeit, ironically, outside the African region. The purpose of the faculty search to which I responded, defining the expectations of my colleagues at UMBC, was cultural diversification of the Psychology Department's graduate enrolment. This institutional goal of diversification was conceived as part of a broad national strategy of redressing inequities of access to education in American society, dating back to President Johnson's 'War on Poverty'. The Provost of UMBC was the African-American groundbreaker, Freeman Hrabowski, who rose to President in the second year of my tenure. His intervention strategy was the Meyerhoff programme (Hrabowski et al., 1998). Its key conceptual focus was on recruiting from high schools around the state African-Americans with high academic performance profiles to enter UMBC as undergraduate students in the fields of science, technology, and mathematics (STEM), and retaining them to graduate with high enough grades to enter graduate study programs in STEM.

Seeking a convergence between my Africa-centred aspirations and the American goals of UMBC, I articulated three strands of implementation: (1) elaborating a graduate student recruitment and admissions process to attract to the programme promising applicants from historically disadvantaged American minority culture groups and from countries abroad with limited higher education opportunities in the field of human development; (2) expansion of the Department's curriculum to include courses with explicit attention to issues of culture; and (3) design of an ambitious, faculty-led research programme in which enrolled graduate students could participate as research assistants while concurrently executing approved studies to qualify for the award of a doctoral degree.

Strand (1) was linked to strand (3) by offering to promising applicants a paid Assistantship on a team research project to which their contribution would qualify them for a Ph.D. The Baltimore Early Childhood Project described in Section 7 provided one of several research-focused frameworks for that linkage from 1992 to 2005. Others were led by Douglas Teti and Kenneth Maton.

Across the programme, the proportion of enrolled students coming from 'minority' cultural backgrounds increased substantially between 1992 and 2002, and most of them completed a Ph.D. degree. Some of the scholars who qualified for the award of the degree in that way went on to conduct independent research and publication in academia (e.g., Danseco, 1997; Ganapathy-Coleman, 2004), while the majority embarked on applied professional careers. In some respects, this diversification of the programme's enrolment contributed to UMBC's broad agenda of enhancing both access to higher education and participation in research in the USA by members of historically disadvantaged groups. Several graduates of African-American heritage (e.g., Adamson-Holley, 1999; Gorham, 2004) went on to apply their expertise to improving the well-being of the African-American sector of the national population. However, many of the graduates classified as 'minority' when joining the programme, after completing earlier stages of their education abroad (Ethiopia, India, Japan, Nigeria, Palestine, the Philippines) went on to situate their post-doctoral careers in North America, contributing to the ongoing global South-North 'brain drain'. Thus, from a multinational perspective, my active recruitment of promising scholars of majority-world origin to enrol in a programme of advanced studies at a minority-world institution could be construed as intensifying an ongoing brain drain, that unjustly deprives nations in the majority world of their best minds while enriching with diversification the already privileged nations of the minority world. The tension between diversifying the science and practices of more industrialised nations in the 'Global North' or 'Minority World', and retention of high-power, creative minds within the economically needy nations of the 'Southern, Majority World' remained a challenge I was better placed to address when I relocated from the USA to Zambia.

Engagement as the Head of a Public Institution

Two dramatic public images stand out in my memory of this 4-year period of my life. In the first I am parading solemnly at the end of a colorful procession led by traditional drummers to mark the opening of a graduation ceremony. In the second I am standing on the balcony of a student residence, deciding whether to drink from a bottle of water being proffered to me by a rioting student.

Graduation ceremonies of UNZA and its various affiliated colleges were joyful occasions attended by large crowds of students and their families.

I used my duty to preside at them as an opportunity to publicise my views on the significance of higher education for Zambian society. In my four annual addresses, I highlighted the themes 'Higher Education and Social Responsibility', 'Nurturing the spirit of inquiry' (Serpell, 2004), 'Social complexity and inclusion', and 'Public accountability of the University', illustrating their application to UNZA as philosophical justifications for the institution's policy and practices. The bottle of water scenario illustrated a less benign, widely attributed role of an African VC, known as 'putting out fires'. The university campus had been experiencing an acute water crisis, and I was relieved to learn from the Resident Engineer that the problem had been rectified. A group of students came to my office and urged me to address a riotous crowd that had assembled near the residences. When I announced that the water supply had been tested and was now safe to drink, someone passed a bottle of water to me and invited me to drink it as proof. I reached out for the bottle, but one of the student leaders beside me snatched the bottle away, exclaiming that we didn't know where the water in it was drawn from. Apparently the rumour that circulated about this incident claimed that I did drink the water, and this was widely cited in my favour ! Both of those settings invited me to deploy oratory and dramatisation to achieve my communicative goals, drawing on my youthful experience in theatre. But I doubted the legitimacy of that approach for responsible leadership, and I did my best to use it sparingly. Three more abstract dimensions of the institution became a focus of my leadership efforts over the course of my four-year term as Vice-Chancellor (VC).

Financial Protection of Institutional Priorities

It was widely known in Zambian society that UNZA was broke, with dilapidated infrastructure, and a massive burden of debt accumulated over the preceding two decades. The last two Vice-Chancellors had been hounded out of office by academic staff dissatisfied with the inability of the institution to cushion them against the adversities of the nation's economic recession. The official responsibilities of the VC included both academic and financial administration, and I felt very ill-prepared for the latter. Pressure of alarming intensity came from five stakeholder groups: three staff unions, retirees, and students, all competing for a share of the very limited funds at the institution's disposal. Given the dim prospects of securing additional funds, I concentrated on strategic financial management. A key concept was **legally ring-fenced financing**. This first came to my attention with respect to a substantial international grant for infrastructure rehabilitation. Later we were able to apply it to a smaller international grant for quality assurance, which we distributed across recruitment of external examiners from abroad, in-house support for research through peer-reviewed competition, and publication of teaching resources. The legal text of the ring-fence provided protection for what I held to be institutional priorities against strident competing demands from aggrieved stakeholders.

Affirmative Action to Enhance Equity of Access

Returning to UNZA after a decade of economic recession, I observed that a conspicuous consumer class of students from wealthy families had emerged, that I didn't recall from the 1970s and 1980s. Reflecting on the underlying causes, I turned my attention to the high schools from which students were entering UNZA and noted that schools located along Zambia's more industrialised 'line-of-rail' seemed to be over-represented. So I proposed to the University Senate that we test a hypothesis, grounded in my research on assessment at lower levels of the school system (Serpell, 1993a, Section 7), that the national Grade 12 exam was a less valid measure of academic potential among rural than urban candidates. I opened my case with an appeal to the senators' personal experiences. Many of them, now senior faculty with advanced degrees, had been among early entrants to UNZA from rural secondary schools in the 1970s and 1980s, and had outperformed classmates entering from urban secondary schools, qualifying for competitive admission to a graduate study programme abroad. Most of their old schools were not doing so well these days, with dilapidated buildings, scarcity of books and a shortfall of qualified teachers due to elites' reluctance to work in a rural area devoid of modern amenities. Under such circumstances, would an intelligent youth have the same chance of scoring high enough at Grade 12 to qualify for a place at UNZA as equally intelligent youngsters attending school in a city on the line of rail? The senators did not need much persuasion to approve the idea that we introduce, on a trial basis, an affirmative admissions programme to accept applicants from rural schools with lower Grade 12 scores than applicants from urban schools. Starting in 2005, we increased the number of offers at each school that had in recent years secured admission for none or very few of their Grade 12 school-leavers. Admission was offered to each of those schools' top three scoring applicants, provided they had scored within the range of overall admissible grades. A total of 750 such affirmative action admissions were made over the first three years, and analysis of their UNZA course grades revealed that their 'academic success rates were not significantly different from those of students admitted on the normal competitive basis without affirmative action' (Serpell & Simatende, 2016, p. 13).

Quality Assurance

University education is sometimes perceived by economists as overpriced, a notion invoked by the World Bank (1988) to urge African governments to shift priority budget allocations away from higher education and to expanding access to basic schooling. My preferred counterargument was to insist that a university's relatively high cost per student compared with other types of school is justified by its provision of opportunities for students to interact with scholars engaged in generating new knowledge (Serpell, 2004). UNZA's distinctive mission, in addition to instruction in existing bodies of established knowledge, was to serve as an incubator for generating new relevant knowledge. Hence, unlike high school teachers, university faculty were expected to devote time and effort to research and publication. Their appointments were made on the strength of academic qualifications, largely based on the candidate's performance as a researcher. Yet, once they were appointed, the institution had no systematic way of monitoring their research performance, except for promotion across the academic ranks, a process entrusted to committees of peers. The bird's-eye view afforded by the office of VC sensitised me to the danger of treating academic disciplines as specialised guilds. I sought, as convenor of various decision-making committees to highlight the complementarity of different types of knowledge in contributing to public service. In moderating applications for promotion within the university's academic ranks, I encouraged reliance on external assessors and universalistic indicators such as the H index as quality criteria that can be understood across disciplines and on the international stage.

Lessons Learned

In the four episodes of engagement at the interface between science and policy described in this section, I repeatedly encountered the challenge of cooperative communication between experts and managers. In the ZNCRDC, the national government turned to its university for expert guidance in the form of a Technical Support Team. The team interpreted the campaign's findings as implying the need for a radical change in the design of existing services. But the government chose instead to continue along a path defined by familiar institutions and professional practitioners. David (1994) has explained how path-dependency is an intrinsic feature of institutions that informs their notoriously slow implementation of change. The Child-to-Child approach to health education adopted at Kabale school demonstrated that outreach activities and group study methods enriched learner outcomes without undermining individual academic progress. But the managers of curriculum development have been reluctant to scale up the approach. Ultimately, perhaps the most important lesson I learned from my brief spells of public responsibility was that good decisions taken in the seat of power depend as much on pragmatic consider-ations as they do on theoretical ones – a sobering thought for a mere theorist on the sideline. If progressive social change is the highest priority for humanity, scholars need to find the humility to acknowledge the situatedness of their expertise and to negotiate consensus among diverse stakeholder groups (Serpell, 2020) (see Figure 12).

9 Searching for Integrity

When I first conceived the project of this Element, I was driven by a desire to build a meaningful connection between the story of my personal life and the published findings of my research. Reflecting on salient features of my childhood and adolescence suggested to me that some of the conclusions about life I had reached as an adult were foreshadowed in my earlier thinking, which was largely devoid of systematic reasoning. Was my stubborn insistence at age five on sounding out Buchanan my own way (Section 2) an early expression of my adult impatience with orthodoxy and bureaucracy? Was my intuitive empathy at age nine with the German cleaner's resentment of her employer's inconsiderateness (Section 2) an early expression of my later political inclination towards solidarity with the oppressed? The narratives of earlier Sections have described the eco-cultural niches of my childhood and adolescence in post-War England, and of my emerging and early adulthood in post-colonial Singapore and Zambia. To what extent did systemic features of the societal and historical contexts of that itinerary influence the kind of person I became and the values to which I now subscribe? Their influence, I believe, was mediated by selective group membership and by institu-tional frameworks, some of which I appropriated, whereas I rejected and some-times challenged others.

Social Groups and Their Intimate Cultures

In earlier sections, I have tried to reconstruct my evolving sense of self in relation to society. Who am I? What am I doing here? My earliest answers to those questions were anchored in the family of which I was a young member in Barnes (Section 2). The answers in my personal diaries were anchored in my adolescent peer group and the curriculum at Westminster school (Section 3). In Singapore and Oxford, as an emerging adult, I began to assert my identity as a nomadic citizen of the world (Section 4). My personal relationships and societal roles generated a system of linguistic and cultural meanings of which I was an insider and owner.

In Barnes, the Serpell family were bound by a sense that we were resident insiders but not confined socioculturally to the mainstream of British, post-war suburbia. Our cultural frame of reference included aesthetic appreciation of European music and visual art and of the French and German languages and literature (Section 2). At Westminster, my peer group were steeped in the Western culture of the school's classics curriculum. Although we were largely compliant with its disciplinary code, we bonded with in-group loyalty to resist what we perceived as unjust use of violence to enforce discipline, both by student monitors and by the Headmaster (Section 3). In the universities of Singapore and Oxford I felt marginal and only joined particular social groups for short-term projects such as theatrical productions or political undertakings including JACARI's survey of colour prejudice in student accommodation (Section 4).

Joining an institution meant participating in the definition of its values and practices: HDRU in Lusaka (1965–1968); Manchester University's HARC (1971–1972); LCHC (in New York in 1976 and later via internet with occasional visits in San Diego in the 1980s and 1990s (http://lchcautobio.ucsd.edu); UNZA's IAS 1977–1983; the ADP programme and Early Childhood Project at the University of Maryland, Baltimore County (1989–2002); and the Psychology Department of UNZA (1972–1976; 1983–1989; 2006–2018). Each of those social groupings had its own intimate culture that bound its members together and mediated the influence on our behaviour of broader, encompassing sociocultural systems. By 1968, it had become apparent to me that HDRU's goals of laying scientific foundations for understanding human development in Zambia were inextricably tied up with the goals of the emerging national university and those of the new nation state, both of which should be determined by its citizens. As such, I found my status as an expatriate anomalous and declared my aspiration to become a Zambian citizen.

Institutions

The academic institutions that framed my professional activities in Lusaka, Manchester, and Baltimore over the decades from 1965 to 2018 each had their own intimate culture to which I was an explicit contributor. In the early years of HDRU I co-constructed with Jan Deregowski a robustly egalitarian mode of peer review through which we offered one another constructive criticism, unburdened by restraint from consideration for the author's feelings. In Manchester, the HARC community of scholarship articulated, under the leadership of Peter Mittler, a shared commitment to the well-being of persons with intellectual disabilities and their families, which served as common ground across our very diverse intellectual styles.

The Psychology Department at UNZA was staffed exclusively by expatriate faculty for its first few years, including Douglas Bethlehem, Richard Schuster, Phillip Kingsley, and myself, numbering fewer than five at any one time. We all shared a commitment to Africanisation that only slowly became a reality during the 1980s and 1990s. Thereafter, the staffing grew to thirteen positions by 2016, almost entirely Zambian citizens, mostly indigenous, a majority of whom had a Ph.D. degree. Just how African culture should be represented in the undergraduate curriculum has been a subject of debate from time to time (Mwanalushi & Ng'andu, 1981; Peltzer & Bless, 1989; Serpell, Chansa-Kabali, & Mwaba 2013), while the emphasis on local applications remains a hallmark of the graduate studies programme. During my spell in the office of the Vice-Chancellor I had opportunities to expand the visibility of the Department's vision and international collaborations that enabled its implementation across the School of Humanities and other Schools of the University. In that way I was able to reciprocate some of the personal growth in breadth of perspective I derived from participation in the institution's activities by contributing to the design of progressive institutional policies. Enduring consequences in UNZA's institutional culture include the affirmative action programme to enhance equity of access to higher education, co-supervision of doctoral degree research by local and international experts, and recourse to internationally developed indicators of research quality for validation of the research profiles of faculty aspiring for promotion.

At UMBC, my mandate on appointment to the Psychology Department included cultural diversification of the curriculum, and gave rise over the twelve years of my sojourn there to three new courses, one graduate and two undergraduate, which continued to be offered after I left (Psyc 230, *Psychology and culture*; Psyc 330, *Child development and culture*; and Psyc 653, *Cultural aspects of human development*). An analysis of the impact of Psyc 330 concluded that 'synthesizing a multicultural classroom with a multicultural syllabus compels students to confront their own intellectual ethnocentrism, diversifies intellectual experience and, for minority students, addresses an intellectual lacuna that they may not yet have articulated' (Ganapathy-Coleman & Serpell, 2008). Other aspects of my interaction with the institution centred on broadening the range of cultural origins from which new graduate students were admitted to the Applied Developmental Psychology programme (discussed in Section 7).

Beginnings of Moral and Political Awareness

In the Barnes family that raised me as a child, moral socialisation was mostly framed in terms of reasoning, with little or no appeal to authoritative texts. But I was also encouraged to participate in other, less anarchic, social activities, including Sunday School and Cub Scouts. It was not until adulthood that I became aware of significant differences between my father's and mother's ideological dispositions and how they framed my early encounters with people from various sociocultural backgrounds. They shared a strong humanistic commitment to religious and international tolerance and regarded themselves as citizens of post-Second World War Western Europe. As I emerged from childhood, I was aware of some aspects of the macro-culture in which my niche was embedded: that England and France were recovering from the second world war, that their respective national languages had international prestige, that their character had been formed over many centuries and was linked in some way to German, but also to Latin and ancient Greek. I was also dimly aware of the Cold War between the West and the USSR, but had little or no interest in its ideological history.

In my adolescence came the exhilarating realisation that all things are logically possible – what Piaget interpreted as 'formal operational thinking'. This was accompanied by the emergence of a psychological interior, a sense of the person I was becoming, that I owned and could divulge as and when I thought fit. During my four years at Westminster school, I began to reflect on how my personal experiences and plans were related to broad societal issues through philosophy, religious faith, and moral commitment.

College in the late 1950s had its own intimate culture, infused with themes from the whole school, and from the wider society of Britain in that era. While appropriating that culture, the cohort that I joined added some refinements, which may or may not have survived the succession of cohorts who followed us. But it certainly influenced my own moral and epistemological orientation, including a belief that rules are made by people interacting in communities, and that when they appear unjust, valid opportunities to challenge them include rational discourse, open confrontation through civil disobedience, and constructive deviations that set an example for others to follow. I left school in a state of rebellion against the hypocrisy of using violence to enforce discipline in a community devoted to the egalitarian pursuit of truth.

My transition from childhood into responsibilities of adulthood was prompted by contradictions encountered as an adolescent at boarding school and as an emerging adult in Singapore (1961–1962), in London (1962), and at Oxford (1962–1965), and culminated in marriage, migration, professional employment and a beginning of parenthood at the age of twenty-one. In Section 4, I reflect on the processes through which I began to take responsibility, in my personal life as a lover, as a self-supporting wage-earner, and as a political activist. A major strand of that transition was the formation of a new interpersonal relationship. Esther and I fell in love in Singapore and exuberantly celebrated our partnership. I made a commitment of long-term loyalty to our union, which was intensified by intergenerational conflict with my parents and sustained as a source of emotional confidence over the next decade, as I embarked on responsibilities of political activism, international migration, and parenting. The eventual collapse of our marriage in Zambia prompted me to reappraise my emerging social identity. The conceptual foundations of my professional research were reframed in the context of embarking on a new, more egalitarian marriage, embedded in Zambian society.

Principles that Emerged Over the Course of My Life Journey

As a child, I took for granted the validity of my parents' values (kindness, generosity, rationality, and tolerance) and judged my own and others' behaviour in terms of them. Only in adolescence did I begin to recognise that those values were not universally shared by all adult human beings. And only in adulthood did I seek to understand systematically why individuals and groups who do broadly share them nevertheless come up with such diverse and seemingly incompatible ways of applying them in their ostensible behaviour.

Later phases of my life-journey took me to various institutional contexts in which I discovered new frames of reference for justifying principles that I had previously accepted passively. In some cases, the context might be said to have moulded my outlook; in others it provoked critical appraisal and sometimes outright resistance. At Westminster, as an adolescent, I rebelled against the use of corporal punishment. Next, as an emerging adult, in the newly independent state of Singapore, I experienced transformative anti-colonial political conscientization. This underpinned my conflict with my father and prompted a new phase of individual independence. At Oxford University in England, I received a sophisticated introduction to the disciplinary perspectives of experimental psychology and Western philosophy. Concurrently, I participated in student activism directed at combating racism and colonialism.

My legally adult life began at the age of 21 with migration to Zambia as a fledgling researcher in the newly established national university of a newly independent African state, concurrently with embarking on the challenging personal–social projects of marriage and parenthood. My intellectual encounter in this period with African culture was narrowly constrained by doctoral research in the tradition of experimental psychology. Serendipitously, during my brief return to Britain in 1971–1972, I gained exposure to the challenge of practical application of cognitive psychological theory in the 'real world', with a focus on children with severe intellectual disability. The seeds of my interest in that topic bore fruit a decade later in Zambia in the National Campaign to

Reach Disabled Children, that confronted me seriously with the challenges of research-based intervention in society and advocacy (Section 8).

Different Ways of Knowing

Growing up bilingual in my childhood, it was apparent to me that the French and English languages followed systematically different rules of grammar and phonology and represented the world with different vocabularies that were only sometimes directly translatable word for word. By the time I left the Lycee at the age of twelve, I was also conscious of deeper and more subtle differences between English and French cultures, informed by a mixture of literature and personal experiences. I felt a sense of ownership/membership as an insider to French culture, and an intuitive authority to interpret nuances of the language, that declined over the years of my adolescence and emerging adulthood. When I visited France as a guest lecturer in my thirties, I found that my pronunciation still enabled me to pass for a native-speaker of French on first encounter, but I struggled to keep going when a conversation deepened. I often resorted to the apologetic self-description: 'J'ai l'accent d'un francais, mais le vocabulaire d'un enfant francais'.

At Westminster, my introduction to classical Latin and Greek included attention to subtleties of the languages, notably through the activity of translation. But I never attained the degree of confident understanding of those cultures that had made French so accessible in my childhood, nor indeed did I ever acquire a sense of ownership of German, which I learned to pronounce by conversational immersion during my holiday visits to Germany in adolescence. But I was always aware due to my early experience with French that 'other' languages are capable of expressing profound aspects of human experience in ways that are different from my familiar ways of knowing in English. Many of my closest friends in later years were profoundly bilingual or plurilingual, having grown from a non-European family of origin into secondary and higher education in either English or French. Individual plurilingualism is taken for granted in many parts of the world, and for me at least it seems to have been a valuable ingredient in the development over my life of an understanding of otherness. Fifty years after the attainment of political sovereignty by the majority of African states, a growing number of indigenous scholars are articulating in the spheres of curriculum development and educational policy the revolutionary insight eloquently epitomised by Prah and Brock-Utne (2009) as 'Multilingualism: an African advantage'.

It was not until my thirties and forties that I began to reach back and reflect on the aesthetic approach to language and the arts in which I was socialised in childhood and adolescence, in search of something that was missing from my scientific use of English in my research and writing for publication. The impetus for this came from recognising the inadequacy of my rigorous, scientific methodology for illuminating the inherent rationality of rural African parents' construal of the exogenous public school curriculum (Section 6). My analysis in terms of perspectivism (Serpell, 1990) led me to problematise the hegemony of Western culture in the formulation of progressive social policy in Zambia and elsewhere in Africa, and eventually to start seeking programmatically to bridge between that cultural worldview and alternative ways of knowing endogenous to marginalised communities (Serpell, 2007, 2020) (see Figure 12).

Aesthetic Appreciation

My personal investment in aesthetic appreciation of the visual arts and music reached a climax in adolescence, alongside a deep interest in literary form. In architecture, I was deeply moved by the Parthenon temple during our school trip to Greece, noting in my diary 'never before have I been so awed, so overpowered by a building'. Yet it was beyond me to characterise or explain my emotional reaction. Many years later I had a similar experience when visiting the *Taj Mahal* at Agra. I have also been overwhelmed by sights of great natural beauty: *Mosi-o-tunya*, the mighty waterfalls on the Zambezi River near Livingstone, visited many times over the years since 1966, the Grand Canyon in Arizona (1999), and sunset over Table Mountain in Cape Town (2009, 2016).

Knowing that something is beautiful has a similar kind of certainty as knowing that one is in love. It is grounded in one's personal sense of self. I acquired that dimension of identity in early adolescence, and in the case of love I discovered in early adulthood how unreliable it was as a ground for action. But I never lost confidence in my capacity for aesthetic appreciation. As the art historian Gombrich (1960, p. 276) observed, a painter 'enriches our experience because he offers us an equivalence within his medium that may also "work" for us'. An innovative artistic creation impresses an audience because the artist offers a comparison that works, but works for whom? And how does it work? Impressionism and cubism could not have earned widespread admiration in Western culture without the traditions of representation that preceded them. Although many modern scientists insist that their technical judgements of theoretical validity are strictly grounded in rational appraisal of empirical evidence, I believe that, in practice, the selection and validation of explanatory models in psychology involve a convergence of four complementary types of criterion, one of which is 'cultural preoccupations' (see Figure 11). Some of those preoccupations can be rationalised as arising from events in the 'real world' such as the

Theoretical preoccupations

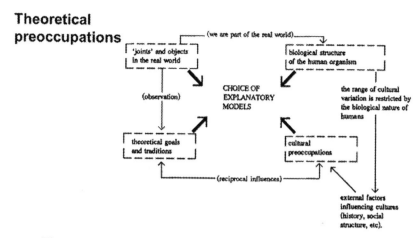

Figure 11 Validation criteria for theoretical models in psychology
(diagram from Serpell, 1990)

proliferation of modern technology. Others, such as human control over nature are more deeply embedded in the culture that flowered in the European Renaissance.

Biculturation

Biculturation was an effortlessly acquired disposition in my childhood, as I commuted between the particular social worlds of my family home and the Lycee. Its implications for the broader sociopolitical principles of **tolerance** and **inclusion** became cumulatively apparent to me over a number of significant life events and challenges. When some of my dorm-mates at Westminster insisted that Hitler could never have gained popular support in English society, I detected a monocultural bias that I did not share. I was just as horrified as my peers by the atrocities of the Holocaust documented in the paperback book *The Scourge of the Swastika* (Russell, 1955) that circulated among us in the dorm. But I saw their protestations as an unworthy attempt to psychologise a societal process. The English, I maintained, a group of which we were all members, were just as vulnerable to psychological aberrations as the Germans. I had met and lived with some Germans in post-war Germany, and they were ordinary human beings just like us.

My experience of racial prejudice in Singapore brought home to me how limited was the scope of my parents' British liberal tolerance. Prejudice, I realised, was a cognitive error to which all people are susceptible. When I witnessed the rise of neo-Nazi fascism in Britain during my years at Oxford, I was shocked but not completely disoriented. I saw it as an internal social disease that English society needed to combat. I was hopeful that its fundamental flaws could and would be exposed by contrary social movements spearheaded by respected mainstream spokespersons, grounding their opposition in the belief that people of diverse cultural origins can coexist peacefully, and show one another respect.

That optimistic view declined over succeeding decades, first with a growing sense that I no longer belonged in England, and a determination to negotiate a legitimate sense of membership in Zambian society. As I reflected on the enduring 'superiority complex' of the mainstream English culture, manifested not only in antiquated formulations surviving from the Victorian Empire and sustained by British colonial practices, but also in arrogant attempts to dominate international discourse relative to French in Europe, Canada and West Africa and relative to Spanish in the USA and Latin America, I began to lose faith in the inherent rationality of the educational curriculum in which I had been immersed at Westminster and Oxford. The irrational, standard orthography of English spelling that was stoutly defended even by indigenous Africans, whose mastery of the language, and hence of the entire school curriculum had ostensibly been frustrated in unnecessary ways by its opacity, came to appear anomalous in more than a trivial way. And I began to realise that rather than the 'unmarked', 'default' solution to universal human problems, the English way was better understood as a socio-historically situated way of addressing challenges that had been differently addressed by other cultural groups, sometimes more successfully than the English way, sometimes less.

Violence, Power, and Responsibility

My initial exposure to interpersonal violence as a boy in the boxing ring gave rise to a strong emotional reaction. The act of violating someone's personal space by imposing force to inflict pain struck me as aesthetically repulsive, and I resolved to avoid participating in social activities such as combative, contact sports that legitimised and encouraged such acts. A few years later, I saw how power was invoked to justify such acts in the name of discipline, and realised that this was not confined to boys but also extended to mature adults in positions of authority (like the Headmaster at Westminster). This impressed me as an abuse of power that disrespected the dignity and personal agency of the victim, undermining the possibility of egalitarian discourse, a fundamental prerequisite to rational communication and authentic cooperation. So I took a stand against violence, first by intimidating the adult agent poised to abuse his power again, and later by declining a position of authority within a system of rules that legitimised violent punishment.

As a student in Oxford, while exploring the potential of activism as a way of challenging political oppression, I came across the moral logic of *satyagraha* (nonviolent resistance), a central philosophical theme of Gandhi's political practice: that which is untrue or unjust must be actively resisted in the form of protest, but without any acts of violence. When I learned of the decision in South Africa by Mandela and others to depart from the principles of *satyagraha* adopted by the African National Congress (ANC) under Luthuli's leadership, I was initially disappointed. However, I suppressed my deeper commitment to pacifism in my eagerness to support the cause of liberation through the anti-apartheid movement. The armed struggle against the oppressive apartheid regime continued throughout my first two decades of life in Zambia, and I befriended a number of ANC activists there. The Zambian government quietly sheltered and encouraged ANC revolutionaries, but stopped short of committing direct military support. So I was never faced with the ultimate dilemma of whether to sign up for military service in the name of a cause I believed in, or to declare myself a conscientious objector.

My first taste of the power that comes with a position of social responsibility was in the form of acting appointments as Head of Department and Director of the Institute at UNZA. My excitement with increased agency for getting things done was moderated by a preference for consensus building with colleagues. Leadership, I found, even in my more substantive positions as Director of the graduate studies programme at UMBC and as Vice-Chancellor of UNZA, was easier to achieve through persuasion than by authoritarian control. The jocular characterisation of the job of a Vice-Chancellor as 'herding cats' rests on the false premise that a university's intimate culture includes a commitment to sticking together, whereas in reality the freedom to disagree is a shared ideological principle of academia. Building on precedent and invoking the organization's principles became my preferred ways of resisting divisive opposition while mobilising progressive social and institutional change.

Engagement with Sociocultural Change

The role of technical support team leader for the Campaign to Reach Disabled Children called for executive decisions when designing record forms, setting up training courses for the Ascertainment Officers, recruiting input from specialists, and other similar tasks. But responsibility for management of implementation of the campaign plan (including disbursement of funds) lay with the national government, which was ultimately accountable to the general public for its success or failure. The disappointing reluctance of government officials to press ahead with implementation of the rationally justified policy shift towards CBR was a lesson for me in how decisions in the 'real world' are often driven by technically extrinsic considerations, overriding scientific ones.

At UMBC, as director of the doctoral studies programme, I participated in consensus-building deliberations within the Department's tradition of reasoned debate, and found reassurance in the widespread willingness to entertain new initiatives while subjecting their implementation to systematic evaluation. As Vice-Chancellor of UNZA for a hectic four years, I carried a wider range of responsibilities than in any other phase of my life. I also had a stronger support team to guide my decision-making than in any of my other work settings. I learned that moral accountability can be shared. Taking on responsibility for leadership of the university brought me, not to a culmination of my academic career, but to a kind of maturity similar to that of parenting. I interpreted my role as facilitating the emergence of a more nuanced and more inclusive national conversation about the relation between academic excellence and public service (twin themes of the university's motto: Service and Excellence).

Personal Integrity

Surrounded by structures, forces, and trends greater than me, pushed and pulled by others, which way should I turn ? How can I claim any decisions as my own ? It is in detailed sequences of behaviour, projects and plans that I am aware of my agency. 'I am because we are' (a maxim of Bantu wisdom). But also, I am now because of where I have been and, hopefully, where I am going. Where I am headed is often ill-defined, and almost infinitely open to revision, constrained by

Figure 12 Multiple stakeholders' funds of knowledge
(diagram from Serpell, 2020).

unknown future contingencies. Yet, as I reach out to interact with others, I sense that some of them recognise me – a person with whose eccentricities they are familiar, as I am of theirs. Our mutual acknowledgment sets in motion a mini-project for each of us. Embedded though we are in a multidimensional system of current traffic flows, social norms and laws, physical constraints, nevertheless you can affect me as an individual, and I can affect you. Dyadic communication with another person varies according to our relationship (family members, friends, colleagues, partners), and is co-constructed in accordance with moral principles of trust, commitment and loyalty which qualify the ways in which the personal relationship is maintained over time. Hence, the bottom line of these reflections on my life-journey across diverse contexts is that the person I am is a result of decisions taken in interaction with other individuals in the past and is informed by my intentions for the future.

References

Adamson-Holley, D. (1999). *Personal dimensions and their relation to education: A follow-up study of students graduating from the Child-to-Child program in Mpika, Zambia.* Baltimore, MD: University of Maryland Baltimore County, Psychology Dept. PhD dissertation.

Akkari, A., Serpell, R., Baker, L., & Sonnenschein, S. (1998). An analysis of teacher ethnotheories. *The Professional Educator, 21,* 45–61.

Apple, M. W. (2014). *Official knowledge: Democratic education in a conservative age.* London: Routledge.

Baker, L. Mackler, K. , Sonnenschein, S., & Serpell, R. (2001). Parents' interactions with their first-grade children during storybook reading and relations with subsequent home reading activity and reading achievement. *Journal of School Psychology, 38,* 1–24.

Banda, F. , Mtenje, A. , Miti, L. et al. (2008). *A unified standard orthography for Southcentral African languages (Malawi, Mozambique and Zambia).* (2nd, revised ed.). Cape Town, South Africa: Centre for Advanced Studies of African Society (Monograph Series No. 229).

Bluma, S., Shearer, M., Frohman, A., & Hilliard, J. (1972). *The Portage Guide to Early Education* (experimental ed.). Wisconsin: Portage.

Booth, T., & Ainscow, M. (2016). *The index for inclusion: A guide to school development led by inclusive values.* Bristol: Centre for Studies on Inclusive Education

Boykin, A. W. (1985). The triple quandary and the schooling of Afro-American children In U. Neisser (ed.), *The school achievement of minority children* (pp. 57–92) Hillsdale, NJ: Erlbaum.

Broadbent, D. E. (1961). *Behavior.* New York: Basic Books

Bronfenbrenner, U. (1979). *The ecology of human development.* Cambridge, MA: Harvard University Press.

Bronfenbrenner, U. (2005). Interacting systems in human development. Research paradigms: present and future (1988). In U. Bronfenbrenner (ed.), *Making human beings human: Bioecological perspectives on human development* (pp. 67–93). Thousand Oaks, CA: Sage.

Chomsky, N. (1965). Aspects of the theory of syntax. Cambridge, MA: MIT Press.

Cole, M. (1985). The zone of proximal development: Where culture and cognition create each other. In J. V. Wertsch (ed.), *Culture, communication, and cognition: Vygotskian perspectives* (pp. 146–161). Cambridge: Cambridge University Press.

Colson, E. (1971). *The social consequences of resettlement: The impact of the Kariba resettlement upon the Gwembe Tonga*. Manchester: Manchester University Press.

Cummins, J. (2019). The emergence of translanguaging pedagogy: A dialogue between theory and practice. *Journal of Multilingual Education Research 9*, Article 13.

Danseco, E. R. (1997). Building bridges: African-American mothers' and teachers' ethnotheories on child development, child problems, and home school relations for children with and without disabilities. Baltimore, MD: University of Maryland Baltimore County, Psychology Dept. PhD dissertation.

Dasen, P. R., Barthelemy, D., Kan, E. et al. (1985). *Nglouele*, l'intelligence chez les Baoule. *Archives de Psychologie, 53*, 295–324.

David, P. A. (1994). Why are institutions the "carriers of history"?: Path dependence and the evolution of conventions, organizations and institutions. *Structural Change and Economic Dynamics, 5*(2), 205–220.

Douglass, F. (1882). *The Life and Times of Frederick Douglass, 1817–1882*. London: Christian Age

Eisemon, T. O. (1989). Educational reconstruction in Africa. *Comparative Education Review, 33* (1), 110–116.

Fantz, R. L. (1961). The origin of form perception. *Scientific American, 204*(5), 66–73.

Ferguson, C. A. (1959). Diglossia. *Word, 15*, 325–340.

Flavell, J. H. (1963). *The developmental psychology of Jean Piaget*. Princeton: Van Nostrand.

Gallimore, R., Weisner, T. S., Kaufman, S. Z., & Bernheimer, L. P. (1989). The social construction of ecocultural niches: Family accommodation of developmentally delayed children. *American Journal on Mental Retardation, 94*, 216–230.

Ganapathy-Coleman, H. (2004). *Cultural conceptions of the child: a study of Indian American, African American and European American parental ethnotheories*. Baltimore, MD: University of Maryland Baltimore County, Psychology Dept. PhD dissertation.

Ganapathy-Coleman, H. & Serpell, R. (2008). Challenging western hegemony through systematic study of cultural diversity: An undergraduate course on child development and culture. *Intercultural Education, 19*(2), 97–104.

Gandhi, M. K. (1927). *An autobiography, or the story of my experiments with truth* (M. Desai, Trans.). Ahmedabad: Navajivan Publishing House.

García, O., & Wei, L. (2014). *Translanguaging: Language, bilingualism and education*. London: Palgrave Pivot.

Gombrich, E. H. (1960). *Art and illusion: A study in the psychology of pictorial representation*. London: Phaidon.

Gorham, L. F. (2004). *Relationships between children's participation in the Black Church and their academic development: An investigation of the eco-cultural, opportunity to learn, and program quality dimensions of church-based academic support programs*. Baltimore, MD: University of Maryland Baltimore County, Psychology Dept. PhD dissertation.

Gramsci, A. (1992). *Prison notebooks volume 2*. New York, NY: Columbia University Press.

Grigorenko, E. L., Geissler, W. P., Prince, R., Okatcha, F., Nokes, C., Kenny, D. & Bundy, D. (2001). The organisation of Luo conceptions of intelligence: A study of implicit theories in a Kenyan village. *International Journal of Behavioral Development*, 25, 367–378.

Gumperz, J. J. (1977). The sociolinguistic significance of conversational code-switching. *RELC Journal*, *8*(2), 1–34.

Habermas, J. (1975). *Legitimation crisis* (T. A. Mc-Carthy, transl.). Boston, MA: Beacon Press.

Habermas, J. (1984). *Theory of communicative action: Reason and the rationalization of society (Vol. 1)*. (T. A. McCarthy, transl.). Boston, MA: Beacon Press.

Hawes, H., & Scotchmer C. (eds.). (1993). *Children for health*. London: The Child-to-Child Trust, UNICEF.

Hebb, D. O. (1949). *Organization of behavior*. New York: Wiley.

Helander, E., Mendis, P., & Nelson, G. (1980) *Training the Disabled in the Community: an experimental manual on rehabilitation and disability prevention for developing countries*. Geneva: World Health Organisation (WHO).

Hrabowski III, F. A., Maton, K. I., & Greif, G. L. (1998). *Beating the odds: Raising academically successful African American males*. New York, NY: Oxford University Press.

Jahoda, G. (1986). Nature, culture and social psychology. *European Journal of Social Psychology*, *16*, 17–30.

Miles, M. (1985). *Where there is no Rehab plan: A critique of the WHO scheme for community based rehabilitation, with suggestions for future directions*. Peshawar: Mental Health Centre.

Minoura, Y. (1992). A sensitive period for the incorporation of a cultural meaning system: A study of Japanese children growing up in the United States. *Ethos*, *20*(3), 304–339.

Mlama, P. (1991). *Culture and development, the popular theatre approach in Africa.* Uppsala: Scandinavian Institute of African Studies.

Morley, D., & Woodland, M. (1988). *See how they grow: Monitoring child growth for appropriate health care in developing countries.* London: MacMillan.

Mtonga, M. (1980). The drama of Gule Wamkulu. *Unpublished master's thesis.* Legon: University of Ghana, Institute of African Studies.

Mumba, P. (2000). Democratisation of Primary Classrooms in Zambia (A Case Study of its Implementation in a Rural School in Mpika). Paper presented at International Special Education Congress 2000, University of Manchester. www.isec2000.org.uk/abstracts/papers_m/mumba_2.htm.

Mwanalushi, M., & Ng'andu, B. E. (1981). Psychology's contribution to national development in Zambia: past, present and future. *African Social Research*, 32, 55–82.

Mwape, G., & Serpell, R. (1996). Participatory appropriation of health science and technology. Poster presented at the International Conference of the International Society for the Study of Behavioural Development (ISSBD). Quebec, Canada: August, 1996.(*ERIC document* ED417191.htm)

Nabuzoka, D. (ed.) (1986). Reaching disabled *children in Zambia: Reports and other documents on the Zambia National Campaign to Reach Disabled Children.* Lusaka: Institute for African Studies, University of Zambia.

Nsamenang, A. B., & Lamb, M. (1993). The acquisition of socio-cognitive competence by Nso children in the Bamenda Grassfields of Northwest Cameroon. *International Journal of Behavioral Development, 16*(3), 429–441.

Peltzer, K., & Bless, C. (1989). History and present status of professional psychology in Zambia. *Psychology and Developing Societies, 1*(1), 53–64.

Phinney, J. S., & Devich-Navarro, M. (1997). Variations in bicultural identification among African American and Mexican American adolescents. *Journal of Research on Adolescence, 7*(1), 3–32.

Prah, K. K., & Brock-Utne, B. (2009). *Bilingualism: An African advantage.* A paradigm shift in African languages of instruction policies. Cape Town, South Africa: Center for Advanced Studies of African society (CASAS Book Series, No. 67).

Pride, J. B. (ed.) (1983). *The New Englishes.* Rowley, MA: Newbury House.

Pridmore, P. (1996). *Children as health educators: The Child-to-Child approach.* Doctoral dissertation, Institute of Education, University of London.

Pryke, S. (1998). The popularity of nationalism in the early British Boy Scout movement. *Social History, 23*(3), 309–324.

Rogoff, B. (1993). Children's guided participation and participatory appropriation in sociocultural activity. In Wozniak, R. H., & Fischer, K. W. (eds.), *Development in context: Acting and thinking in specific environments* (pp. 121–153). Hillsdale, NJ: Erlbaum.

Russell Lord, E. F. L. (1955). *The scourge of the swastika: A short history of Nazi war crimes* (7th ed.). London, UK: Cassell.

Sam, D. L. (1997). Acculturation and adaptation. *Handbook of cross-cultural psychology, 3*(2), 291–326.

Sam, D. L., Jasinskaja-Lahti, I., Horenczyk, G., & Vedder, P. (2013). Migration and integration: Some psychological perspectives on mutual acculturation [Editorial]. *Zeitschrift für Psychologie, 221*(4), 203–204.

Sameroff, A. J., & Fiese, B. H. (1992). Family representations of development. In I.E. Siegel, A. V. Mcgillicuddy Delisi, & J. J. Goodnow (eds.), *Parental belief systems: The psychological consequences for children*. Hillsdale: Erlbaum

Sandow, S. (1984). The portage project: Ten years on. In T. Dessent (ed.), *What is important about Portage?* Windsor: NFER/Nelson.

Sanson, A. V., Van Hoorn, J., & Burke, S. (2019). Responding to the impacts of the climate crisis on children and youth. *Child Development Perspectives, 13* (4) 201–207.

Serpell, R. (1968). Selective attention and interference between first and second languages. *Institute for Social Research Communication No.4*. Lusaka: University of Zambia.

Serpell, R. (1970). *Chi-Nyanja comprehension by Lusaka schoolchildren: A field experiment in second language learning*. Human Development Research Unit, University of Zambia.

Serpell, R. (1977). Strategies for investigating intelligence in its cultural context. *Quarterly Newsletter of the Institute for Comparative Human Development, 1*(3), 11–15.

Serpell, R. (1978). Learning to say it better: A challenge for Zambian education. In L. N. Omondi & Y. T. Simukoko (eds.), Language and education in Zambia. *Institute for African Studies Communication No. 14* (pp. 29–57). Lusaka: University of Zambia. Reprinted (1983) in abridged form in J. B. Pride (ed.), *The New Englishes*. Rowley, MA: Newbury House.

Serpell, R. (1979). How specific are perceptual skills? A cross-cultural study of pattern reproduction. *British Journal of Psychology, 70*, 365–380.

Serpell, R. (1980). Linguistic flexibility in urban Zambian children. *Annals of the New York Academy of Sciences, 345* (Studies in Child Language and Multilingualism, edited by V. Teller & S. J. White), 97–119.

Serpell, R. (1986). Specialized centres and the local home community: Children with disabilities need them both. *International Journal of Special Education, 1*(2), 107–127.

Serpell, R. (1988). Childhood disability in sociocultural context: Assessment and information needs for effective services. In P. R. Dasen, J. W. Berry & N. Sartorius (eds.), *Health and cross-cultural psychology: Towards applications* (pp. 256–280). Newbury Park, CA: Sage.

Serpell, R. (1990). Audience, culture and psychological explanation: A reformulation of the emic-etic problem in cross-cultural psychology. *Quarterly Newsletter of the Laboratory of Comparative Human Cognition, 12*(3), 99–132. http://lchc.ucsd.edu/Histarch/newsletters.html.

Serpell, R. (1993a). *The significance of schooling: Life-journeys in an African society.* Cambridge: Cambridge University Press

Serpell, R. (1993b). Interface between socio-cultural and psychological aspects of cognition: A commentary. In E. Forman, N. Minick & A. Stone (eds.), *Contexts for learning: Sociocultural dynamics* (pp. 357–368). Oxford: Oxford University Press.

Serpell, R. (1994). Negotiating a fusion of horizons: A process view of cultural validation in developmental psychology, *Mind, Culture and Activity, 1,* 43–68.

Serpell, R. (2001). Cultural dimensions of literacy promotion and schooling. In L. Verhoeven & C. Snow (eds.), *Literacy and Motivation* (pp. 243–273). Mahwah, NJ: Erlbaum.

Serpell, R. (2004). Nurturing the spirit of inquiry. Vice-Chancellor's address to the University of Zambia's Graduation Ceremony. Lusaka: University of Zambia, 11 June 2004.

Serpell, R. (2006). Negotiating the middle ground between the ostensible and shared horizons: A dynamic approach to cross-cultural communication about human development. In J. Straub, D. Weidemann, C. Kölbl, & B. Zielke (eds.), *Pursuit of meaning: Advances in cultural and cross-cultural psychology* (pp. 393–433). Berlin: Verlag.

Serpell, R. (2007). Bridging between orthodox western higher educational practices and an African sociocultural context. *Comparative Education, 43*(1), 23–51.

Serpell, R. (2008). Participatory appropriation and the cultivation of nurturance: A case study of African primary health science curriculum development. In P. R. Dasen & A. Akkari (eds.), Educational Theories and Practices from the "Majority World (pp 71–97). New Delhi: SAGE.

Serpell, R. (2017). How the study of cognitive growth can benefit from a cultural lens. *Perspectives on Psychological Science, 12*(5), 889–899.

Serpell, R. (2020). Culture-sensitive communication in applied developmental research. *Human Development, 64*(4–6), 1–16.

Serpell, R. & Adamson-Holley, D.E. (2016). African socialisation values and non-formal educational practices: child development, parental beliefs and educational innovation in rural Zambia. Chapter 22 (pp 1–25). In T. Abebe, J. Waters (eds.), *Labouring and Learning, Geographies of Children and Young People 10*. New York, NY: Springer Link.

Serpell, R., Baker, L., & Sonnenschein, S. (2005). *Becoming Literate in the City: the Baltimore Early Childhood Project*. New York, NY: Cambridge University Press.

Serpell, R., Baker, L., Sonnenschein, S., & Hill, S. (1991) Caregiver ethnotheories of children's emergent literacy and numeracy. Paper presented at a symposium on the socio-cultural context of development, 11th Biennial Meetings of the *International Society for the Study of Behavioural Development (ISSBD)*. Minneapolis, MN: July, 1991.

Serpell, R., Chansa-Kabali, T., & Mwaba, S. O. C. (2013). *Proposal for a new course on African psychology and/or on Cultural psychology*. Lusaka: University of Zambia, Psychology Department, unpublished document.

Serpell, R., & Deregowski, J. B. (1980). The skill of pictorial perception: an interpretation of cross-cultural evidence. *International Journal of Psychology, 15*, 145–180.

Serpell, R., & Hatano, G. (1997). Education, literacy and schooling in cross-cultural perspective. In J. W. Berry, P. R. Dasen & T. M. Saraswathi (eds.), *Handbook of Cross-Cultural Psychology (2nd ed.), Volume 2* (pp. 345–382). Boston, MA: Allyn & Bacon.

Serpell, R., & Jere-Folotiya, J. (2011). Basic education for children with special needs in Zambia: Progress and challenges in the translation of policy into practice. *Psychology and Developing Societies, 23*(2), 211–245.

Serpell, R., Mumba, P., & Chansa-Kabali, T. (2011). Early educational foundations for the development of civic responsibility: An African experience. In C. A. Flanagan and B. D. Christens (eds.), *Youth civic development: Work at the cutting edge*. Hoboken, NJ: Wiley, pp. 77–93.

Serpell, R., & Nabuzoka, D. (1991) Early intervention in Third World countries. In D. M. Mitchell & R. I. Brown (eds.), *Early intervention studies for young children with special needs* (pp. 93–126). London: Chapman & Hall.

Serpell, R., & Nsamenang, A. B. (2015). The challenge of local relevance: Using the wealth of African cultures in ECCE programme development. In P. T. M. Marope & Y. Kaga (eds.), *Investing against evidence: The global state of early childhood care and education* (pp. 231–247). Paris: UNESCO.

Serpell, R. & Simatende, B. (2016). Contextual responsiveness: an enduring challenge for educational assessment in Africa. *Journal of Intelligence, 4* (1) 3–22.

Serpell, R. & Sneddon, C. (1965). Colour prejudice and Oxford landladies. *Race, 6*(4), 322–333.

Serpell, R., Sonnenschein, S., Baker, L., & Ganapathy, H. (2002). Intimate culture of families in the early socialization of literacy. *Journal of Family Psychology, 16*, 391–405.

Serpell, R., Sonnenschein, S., Baker, L. et al. (1997). Parental ideas about development and socialization of children on the threshold of schooling. *Reading Research Report No. 78.* Athens, GA: NRRC, Universities of Georgia & Maryland College Park). (ERIC document ED 405568.htm).

Seuss (Dr) (1960). *Green Eggs and Ham.* New York, NY: Random House, Beginner Books.

Shapiro, M. B. (1960). The rotation of drawings by illiterate Africans. *Journal of Social Psychology, 52*, 17–30.

Siann, G. (1972). Measuring field dependence in Zambia: A cross-cultural study. *International Journal of Psychology, 7*(2), 87–96.

Sonnenschein, S., Baker, L., & Serpell, R. (1995). Documenting the child's everyday home experiences: The ecological inventory as a resource for teachers. *NRRC Instructional resource No.11.* National Reading Research Center, Universities of Georgia and Maryland.

Sonnenschein, S., Baker, L., Serpell, R., Goddard-Truitt, V., & Munsterman, K. (1997). Parental beliefs about ways to help children learn to read: The impact of an entertainment or a skills perspective. *Early Child Development and Care, 127–8*, 111–118.

Spock, B. (1949). *Dr. Spock's baby and child care.* 9th ed. Mass Market Paperback.

Super, C. M., & Harkness, S. (1986). The developmental niche: A conceptualization at the interface of child and culture. *International Journal of Behavioral Development, 9*, 545–569.

Susser, M. (1990). Disease, illness, sickness; impairment, disability and handicap. *Psychological Medicine, 20*(3), 471–473.

Tuck, S. (2013). Malcolm X's visit to Oxford University: U.S. civil rights, Black Britain, and the special relationship on race. *The American Historical Review, 118*(1), 76–103

Udell, C. L. (2001). *Educational Innovation: A Case Study of Child-to-Child in Zambia.* MA thesis, Psychology Dept. Baltimore, MD: University of Maryland, Baltimore County.

UNESCO (1990). *Education for all.* Jomtien, Thailand: UNESCO,

UNESCO (1994). Salamanca statement and framework for action on special needs education. Retrieved from http://www.unesco.org/education/pdf/ SALAMA_E.PDF (accessed November 2008)

Wechsler, D. (1975). Intelligence defined and undefined: A relativistic appraisal. *American Psychologist, 30*(2), 135.

Wober, M. (1969). Distinguishing centri-cultural from cross-cultural tests and research. *Perceptual and Motor Skills.*

World Bank. (1988). Education in Sub-Saharan Africa: Policies for Adjustment. *Revitalization and Expansion.* Washington, DC: World Bank

Wolfenden Committee. (1957). Report of the Committee on Homosexual Offences and Prostitution. www.parliament.uk/about/living-heritage/transformingsociety/ private-lives/relationships/collections1/sexual-offences-act-1967/wolfenden-report-/.

Cambridge Elements ☰

Psychology and Culture

Kenneth D. Keith

University of San Diego

Kenneth D. Keith is author or editor of more than 160 publications on cross-cultural psychology, quality of life, intellectual disability, and the teaching of psychology. He was the 2017 president of the Society for the Teaching of Psychology.

About the Series

Elements in Psychology and Culture features authoritative surveys and updates on key topics in cultural, cross-cultural, and indigenous psychology. Authors are internationally recognized scholars whose work is at the forefront of their subdisciplines within the realm of psychology and culture.

Cambridge Elements $\equiv$

Psychology and Culture

Elements in the Series

A full series listing is available at: www.cambridge.org/EPAC

Printed in the United States
by Baker & Taylor Publisher Services